Dearest Helen

Remember God is always with you through every peak and valley. Keep your faith alive — you are a lovely woman.

May God Bless you Always!

Thanks for being my mom's best friend. I hope you love the Book.

12-16-2018
xx

Faith Walk

One Woman's Journey to Finding Herself

Angie Montgomery

BALBOA
PRESS
A DIVISION OF HAY HOUSE

Copyright © 2018 Angie Montgomery.

All rights reserved. No part of this book may be used or reproduced by any means, graphic, electronic, or mechanical, including photocopying, recording, taping or by any information storage retrieval system without the written permission of the author except in the case of brief quotations embodied in critical articles and reviews.

NIV: Scriptures taken from the Holy Bible, New International Version®, NIV®. Copyright © 1973, 1978, 1984, 2011 by Biblica, Inc.™ Used by permission of Zondervan. All rights reserved worldwide. www.zondervan.com The "NIV" and "New International Version" are trademarks registered in the United States Patent and Trademark Office by Biblica, Inc.

This book is a work of non-fiction. Unless otherwise noted, the author and the publisher make no explicit guarantees as to the accuracy of the information contained in this book and in some cases, names of people and places have been altered to protect their privacy.

Balboa Press books may be ordered through booksellers or by contacting:

Balboa Press
A Division of Hay House
1663 Liberty Drive
Bloomington, IN 47403
www.balboapress.com
1 (877) 407-4847

Because of the dynamic nature of the Internet, any web addresses or links contained in this book may have changed since publication and may no longer be valid. The views expressed in this work are solely those of the author and do not necessarily reflect the views of the publisher, and the publisher hereby disclaims any responsibility for them.

The author of this book does not dispense medical advice or prescribe the use of any technique as a form of treatment for physical, emotional, or medical problems without the advice of a physician, either directly or indirectly. The intent of the author is only to offer information of a general nature to help you in your quest for emotional and spiritual well-being. In the event you use any of the information in this book for yourself, which is your constitutional right, the author and the publisher assume no responsibility for your actions.

Any people depicted in stock imagery provided by Getty Images are models, and such images are being used for illustrative purposes only. Certain stock imagery © Getty Images.

Print information available on the last page.

ISBN: 978-1-9822-1409-8 (sc)
ISBN: 978-1-9822-1410-4 (hc)
ISBN: 978-1-9822-1411-1 (e)

Library of Congress Control Number: 2018912287

Balboa Press rev. date: 11/06/2018

THE STARS

The stars moved her.
They lit up her soul just as much as the night sky.
They reminded her of how precious life and time and space are.
How it all goes way too fast.
They allowed her to slow life down to a crawl.
To lay in the grass and simply breathe.
Breathe in the past. All that it had shown her.
Breathe in the lilacs in the summer air, the sound of crickets.
The feeling of the cool, wet grass beneath her toes.
She was finally home. At peace with her place in the world.
She looked up at the night sky, closed her eyes and whispered to whoever would listen, "thanks...for all of it."

Contents

Foreword ix
Gratitudes from the Author xi
Preface xiii

Chapter 1   Daddy's Little Girl 1
Chapter 2   Cracked Wide Open 19
Chapter 3   Born to Love 35
Chapter 4   Dream On, Moon Child 45
Chapter 5   The Purpose in Your Calling 65
Chapter 6   Sunshine After the Rain 76
Chapter 7   Kick F-E-A-R to the C-U-R-B 100
Chapter 8   Wild Little Thing 106
Chapter 9   Faith Walk 140
Chapter 10   A Time to Heal 146
Chapter 11   Who Am I? 166

Prayers of Hope 179
Pretty Little Things From My Heart to Yours 183
Afterword from the Author 187

Foreword

There is nothing else like falling in love, and this will be no exception. Allow me to introduce the brightest ray of sunshine you'll ever meet, Angie Montgomery, a dear friend I fondly refer to as my soul sister. As you will soon come to understand, it is easy to fall in love with Angie's genuine nature and her beautiful heart, which you'll find poured into the pages of this book.

Through the last nearly fifteen years of our friendship, I've had the unique opportunity to witness Angie's remarkable journey through life up close and personal. We shared many moments throughout the years, from the thrills of jumping out of an airplane together, to separately moving across the country at the same time. Our strikingly parallel lives have intersected in many ways, and will undoubtedly continue to do so. It's not every day friendships of this magnitude come along.

As a close friend with a front row seat, my heart is full watching Angie's story unfold. The milestones along the way include adventures not for the faint of heart. Watching Angie fearlessly charge forward to achieve her goals and dreams with passion, one might begin to wonder where all this fire comes from. The answer lies within these pages through one woman's unique and insightful perspective.

It isn't all peaches and cream, jelly bean, Angie tells me when life gets hard. She reminds us before the sunshine, there was darkness, pain, loss and grief. Angie shows us that through the most painful moments, hope can be found like a phoenix rising from the ashes, and faith will carry us to places we never thought possible.

My wish for you, dear reader is that you take in this extraordinary woman's reflections on her walk-through life. Breathe it in deeply. Reflect on your own life experiences, your story and from your darkest moments, find hope, courage, and inspiration to move you forward on your own path through this journey we call life. The journey is our home.

Love and Blessings,

Shari Suelter

Gratitudes from the Author

To God, the truest, most precious love of my life. To my Lord and Savior Jesus Christ, my BFF, for walking with me and carrying me when I couldn't carry myself.

To my daddy, Dave Montgomery, for inspiring me to live a fuller life through the loss of your own. You continue to teach me there is nothing in this life to be afraid of except not living the life you were meant to live. Although life has separated us for now, I'll always be your "little girl." I continually wish you were here so I could give you butterfly kisses, a big hug, a squeeze, a handshake and a pat on the back and tell you one more time how much I love you. A day hasn't gone by that I haven't thought about you. Thanks for being my inspiration to fully live while I'm here, to take chances, to stay young in spirit, get joy out of the small things, keep family close, be a friend, step outside my comfort zone, follow my dreams, keep fighting for what I believe in, treat others with kindness, be a good person, take plenty of pictures to remember the moments that make up my life, and to enjoy the company of children. You are missed, and yet I know you're still right here by my side. Knowing you are with grandpa and grandma Montgomery tilling gardens, planting flowers and tinkering with old cars gives me peace.

To my beautiful family for loving me. To my mom, one of my greatest confidantes, I can always count on you to lend a listening ear. To my two God given built in besties, my sister Allison and my brother Mike. Life would never have been the same without you both in it. And to their partners, my bonus siblings, Nate and Wendy, I'm so glad you're part of the family. To my most treasured nephews and nieces, Austin, Annabelle,

Madison, Landon, Maddox, Leo and Myles. Being an auntie and your "Gi Gi" has been one of the absolute best things in my life. To my cousin Tony and dear friend Janette who encouraged me to follow my dreams and supported me when things didn't turn out as planned. You will never know how much that meant to me. To my Uncle Dan for being my dad's twin and leaving a big piece of him here on Earth. You are a second dad to me and for that I'm grateful. To my countless Aunts, Uncles and Cousins who make me feel like home. To Luke, my boo, for being on the journey with me. I'm glad I found you in the aisle of a grocery store. And last, but certainly not least, to my beloved Grandma Alice, who's spirit lives on within me. Thank you for being my cheerleader on the other side and for guiding me along my path. When I said you were my best friend and my favorite person all those times, I meant it, and I still do.

God has certainly blessed me with some amazing women in my life, your friendships have been my refuge more than a time or two. To my soul sister, Shari, thank you for writing the foreword to my book and for the countless hours of talking about God's purpose for our lives and the emergency calls when I was in major doubt and fear mode. And to your wonderful husband, Tim, for the talks when I needed them most. Thank you for living bravely and trusting in the plan. To Flame, who is a coach amongst coaches and a friend amongst friends. You came into my life right when I needed you the most. To Deb C, who understood me in ways most don't by courageously walking your own path in truth and light. To Andrea, for living an authentic journey. To Shannon, for coming into my life as a young girl and then helping to encourage me to finish this book during our time in Colorado and beyond. To Kathy Larsen and her HeartLighters, for giving me so much love and encouragement and making me feel at home. To La Ronda, for the countless talks when I needed them most. And finally, to all the other beautiful souls who have made up the moments in my life, who have taught me lessons my soul longed to learn. You are all loved and adored as brightly as the stars in the sky.

Preface

Footprints in the Sand
By Margaret Fishback Powers
(This poem is dedicated to my Grandma Margaret)

One night I dreamed a dream.
As I was walking along the beach with my Lord.
Across the dark sky flashed scenes from my life.
For each scene, I noticed two sets of footprints in the
sand, one belonging to me and one to my Lord.
He whispered, "My precious child, I love you and will never leave
you never, ever, during your trials and sufferings. When you saw
only one set of footprints, it was then that I carried you."

It's been a long and winding road. It's been five years with this book on my heart. As I sit here tonight, writing my first pages, I'm not sure where this will take me. Nevertheless, I am willing. Willing to share my thoughts, my feelings, my revelations and myself. Only because God wrote it on my heart to do so; to encourage and motivate those around me to live the life of their dreams to be brave and courageous. Therefore, I must be, too. I hope these pages that you are about to embark upon will touch a chord, hit a note and in some small way resonate with you. For that is my wish, my hope, my dream to inspire those around me. It feels good to be at a place where I have lived enough life to be at a point to share my experiences through God's guidance and assistance with writing this book.

This is my story of taking loss and living more fully despite it. We can use our grief to recreate the life we have always wanted to live. I want to provide comfort and solace to those in their darkest moments to press on. Life will be good again and in many ways better than before your loss occurred. It's not always easy to pick up the pieces of what feels like a broken and shattered life, but it is possible. When we can see our darkest, deepest, soul wrenching moments as our greatest gifts we can transform anything we experience into something beautiful. This is my story. I hope it's yours, too.

The book I first intended this to be has evolved over time. I suppose in the same way that we evolve as we continue down our path. What was once a story of encouragement has now become a story of faith and walking in it. May you walk in your own faith to reach your own truth and light. May you find the meaning in the misery, the light in the dark, the wisdom in the journey and the love in the pain.

Chapter One

Daddy's Little Girl

"Those we love don't go away, they walk beside us every day…unseen, unheard, but always near, still loved, still missed and very dear."
- Author Unknown

Here I am writing the first pages of a book that I have only dreamed of beginning until now. Today is the day that I have promised myself I will get serious about writing my story. Partially because writing this book feels like my truest destiny and partially because I want to live a more inspired, authentic life and writing is a big part of that mix. It's not easy starting this story because I'm afraid of sharing myself with the world and yet I know I'm meant to.

So here I am on a cool fall September evening in Omaha, Nebraska writing these first paragraphs from my bed. When the idea of writing about my journey first came to me five years ago, as I was running on the trail, I thought it would feel different. I met God for the first time that day. He spoke to me and I listened. We will get to that later, but for now, where I'm at in my life isn't where I thought I'd end up. I've experienced some high highs and some deep lows in between the time I first dreamed of writing this book and now. Things haven't gone the way I'd hoped and yet I'm still writing. I'm in the midst of a rocky time in my life. But I awake each day in the same situation asking for answers to my prayers and guidance for my struggles. What I continue to hear back is to write. So, write I shall. For me these are the steps I must take to get where I long to go. To become a writer. If you're experiencing your own calling, keep taking the steps to get there, too. Don't stuff your dreams down into the dark instead let them come out into the light of day. Here is my story of how I ended up here and what I'm doing to fight my way out, to find my way even when my spirit feels like giving up. You see it's all part of my journey, of my faith walk.

I often ask myself why I haven't fully stepped out to do what I fully love yet. But then as if by divine guidance I remember that I have. Only a little less than two years ago I left my safe and secure life in Nebraska to follow my dreams to live in Colorado, a move I felt very guided to take. A move that God was beckoning me to take all on my own without the comfort of knowing a single soul. Little did I know this was going to be my time away with nothing except God to lean on for all my needs. A time in my life I can look back on now with gratitude knowing that it turned me into who I was always meant to become. Learning humility in the way only difficult seasons in our lives can teach us. Understanding what it meant to have no one or nothing to rely on except for God.

Before the move to Colorado, I was working for a non-profit organization that I was passionate about, however, leaving seemed pale in comparison to the promise I felt in my heart that this new beginning was going to offer me. I had prayed and prayed on it for months and all signs led to taking this leap of faith. So, I did what anyone who wants to experience a full life did, I followed my heart and risked it all. Leaving the job, I had been at for a decade plus, and jumping into self-employment as a life coach, I decided to really go for it. But this wasn't the beginning of my soul-searching journey, it had begun long before my move to Colorado. My journey of self-discovery began the day my life changed forever.

My story begins on February 18, 2010. It's the best place I know to start. It's where my dad's life ends and where mine simultaneously begins. I will never forget the news, and honestly, I have played it back to myself in my head on many occasions, especially after I first heard the news. Replaying those initial days must be the moments I really want to feel the pain, proving to myself that it was all real, that my dad existed, and that his life mattered. The unrelenting thing about pain is that your memory never allows you to forget. Instead it comes back to it like you are living right in it again, as if you haven't made one step in the direction towards recovery, grieving, healing or whatever you want to call it. When you have such a profound loss, it takes the you, that you were before it happened, away from yourself; most likely never to resurface the same again. Yet you will still long for that person who you were before your world shattered. For me, maybe I wanted to live in that world. It makes me feel like my dad was just here like it was just yesterday that I lost him instead of the days and years piling up since he was last here on Earth, living and breathing right alongside all of us. When my life felt whole.

I'll never forget the day it happened. I guess we're not meant to forget those types of days, that would somehow be too easy on us, if we forget the very moments that shaped who we would become. I woke up that morning like any other morning. I went to work and sat at my desk the majority of the day like any other day. But this day would end up very different. It would change the course of my life in ways I never would have imagined. I got the call that everyone dreads. I was still at work, it was six thirty at night, like any normal Thursday evening, I was busy caught up in the day to day routines that made up my life. I just had that one "last" thing to get done before I would let myself go home for the day like everyone else had done two hours before.

Out of the silence, my cell phone rang, it was my sister. Nothing out of the ordinary there. But when I picked up the call there was something terribly wrong. She was in tears and soon I would be too. All she could muster was that Dad had passed away. The days that followed that fateful call were both heartbreaking and full of love. As the words rang true in my mind, my heart just couldn't fathom the truth I felt in them. I was in such shock that I had to ask her several times if Dad was gone. I found myself unable to sit still, before I knew it, I was up pacing back and forth. Our dad was gone? It was impossible. Not our dad. He was only fifty-six years old. He hadn't been sick and there was no warning.

As soon as I could collect myself, I rushed out of the office. As I left the office, on top of the shock, I felt a sharp tinge of guilt take over. How could

I still be at work when my dad was gone? I had been putting in so many hours at work and not enough time devoted to other areas of my life. Areas that were of equal importance if not more. This would soon be a regret I would grapple with, but somewhere down the road would teach me a very important lesson about balance and choosing our time wisely.

Once I was in the car I rushed to call my husband to tell him the news as if I was on autopilot. Once I got him on the phone I couldn't believe the words that were coming out of my mouth. How was I telling him that my daddy passed away? This wasn't real, was it? Somehow, I thought, I must have fallen deep asleep and conjured up this horrible nightmare. I was going to be able to call my dad just to listen to his voice when I woke up. Wasn't I?

As I drove the twenty miles to be with my family, I couldn't wait to fall into their arms and unzip all the pain I had pent up, letting it all out in one long exhausting cry. Like many low times in our lives my pain wasn't going anywhere any time soon. I quickly learned it would take time and perseverance on my part to get myself back. To heal enough to go on again. Once the sting of the shock wore away, grief would cling to me for months, settling into my bones, telling me it was true, my dad wasn't coming back. Grief would become my constant companion.

Over the next few days, while planning his funeral, I was determined to do all I could to show my dad all the love I had for him. My heart kept telling me to run to him, to find him, and to bring him home. But my reality spoke a different language. One that I was nowhere near ready to accept. The deep yearning, I felt to be with him was at times downright unbearable. All I wanted in the world was to give him the biggest hug and butterfly kiss I could muster, to somehow wake him up with all the love I had for him. It's tough when there are no goodbyes, no way to turn back the clock and create a different outcome. All of a sudden there were no more smiles or laughter or memories to share. It felt like the shock was going to stay forever. My mind was running over and over it again and again. How could this have happened? He was just here and now he is gone.

I've heard stories of other people losing their loved ones with their lives being changed in a split second, but this just couldn't be happening to my family. Could it? I imagined my dad walking through the door and life going on as it should have. I would have my dad back and life would go on as planned. As it was supposed to be with my family together. We all needed him. It just wasn't supposed to happen this way. How could this be? I needed him to continue to guide me. I wasn't ready to say goodbye. I never would be and yet I had no other choice.

As I sat back and looked at the reality of the situation, my dad was only fifty-six years old, making my mom a young widow at fifty-three years old, there was just no way we could live the rest of our lives without him. I had never imagined losing my dad at twenty-nine years old. For goodness sake, I wasn't even thirty yet and hadn't had children of my own. The sobering reality was this meant he wouldn't be there to meet them. And my sister, who was thirty-two years old, had four children who needed their papa around to show them the ropes and to play tickle monster with them until they couldn't handle the laughter any longer. And then to see my brother who was so young, at only twenty-three years old, being forced to deal with such a huge loss was heart wrenching. My brother wasn't married yet and my dad would want to be there for it. It all left me hollow. There was so much more left for my dad to experience and yet I had to try to accept the new reality of our lives. And then, the realization of all realizations, I would never get to see my dad again.

There was so much to do those first few days after his passing. As always with situations such as this you are thrown into the unexpected, and you must hold yourself together, if for no other reason than to honor the memory of the one you love. I poured my heart and soul into my dad's farewell, trying my hardest, along with my family to make it special for him. I understood this would be one of the last earthly displays of my affection for his life here on Earth.

The one thing that comforted me was knowing my dad would be there even if from the other side to experience it with us. To this day I pray my dad was touched and moved knowing how much we loved him and how much his life mattered. During times like these all that's required is doing the best you can. Getting through those days were not easy. I had huge waves of grief rolling in, but suddenly a moment of peace swept over me for the first time in days. The first inkling I had that there was something bigger going on within me began at my dad's viewing. As I was standing next to my dad for one of the final times, spending some precious alone time with him, during the midst of my immense pain, suddenly, this calm came over me, a peace like I'd never experienced before. In that moment, I knew I was literally feeling what my dad felt. This overwhelming feeling of peace was his sign to me that he was okay. This was a miracle to me in a very stormy time. Then just as suddenly as it came over me it dissipated and my sorrow, sadness and brokenness resumed.

Although the moment was fleeting, I recognized it as a gift instantly. The peace I had just felt would be the peace my dad would feel for eternity. It opened me up to believing I could somehow communicate with God, and with my dad on the other side. In that brief, but powerful moment, I knew this was all part of God's plan and although I wasn't close to accepting the loss, at least I knew in my heart that my dad was still there with all of us, if only in a different way.

Since that moment I have never stopped seeking my dad's presence in my life. Knowing that he is with me along my journey, continuing to guide me, brings me great comfort. In my heart, I know my dad is writing this book with me, helping me along the way. And so, began my spiritual awakening to gifts from the other side. I now had a personal connection to what life is like after dying in the physical form. What a true gift.

There are other forms of gifts brought to us during times of sorrow. Words are one of those for me, bringing me deep comfort, during times of difficulty in my life. I want to share two very special poems with you that helped me get through very challenging times. I hope they bring you comfort along your journey towards healing as well.

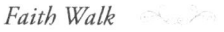

After my dad's passing I was comforted by a poem my Grandma Alice always adored that she left hanging on her wall at home and was ultimately read at her own funeral.

Immortality by Mary Elizabeth Frye

Do not stand at my grave and weep,
I am not there,
I do not sleep,
I am a thousand winds that blow,
I am the diamond glints on snow,
I am the sunlight on ripened grain,
I am the gentle autumn rain.
I am not there, I did not die.

This is another poem that is close to my heart and was read at my dad's service.

Don't Grieve For Me by Shannon Lee Moseley

Don't grieve for me, for now I'm free,
I'm following the path God laid for me,
I took His hand when I heard Him call,
I turned my back and left it all.
I could not stay another day,
To laugh, to love, to work or play,
If my parting has left a void,
Then fill it with remembered joy.

I am writing this book not only for me but for you. If you're going through a loss I want you to know you're not alone. For many months after my dad passed I felt like I was dying myself. I couldn't possibly understand how I was going to make it through without my dad in my life. Grief has a way of flipping our world upside down and it is important to feel all our emotions. On the other side of grief there is more life for you to live. I want to share how you can turn your grief into glory, your suffering into peace, your tragedy into triumph, your loss into joy.

truth is there really are no words for the hole you feel in your heart. I didn't have any words to fully describe the pain I was in those first few days, let alone the sorrow that would follow me as if it were my new shadow. Wherever I went, my grief wasn't far behind, reminding me that it was going to require me to take a long and hard look at my own life before it would saunter off into the sunset.

Feel your pain, allow yourself to be angry, sad, yell, scream do what you must. Don't stuff it down or tell yourself you should be doing better before you're ready to do better.

I remember sitting up at night when I should have been long asleep crying out to God, "not my dad…no…not my dad…please God no." This soon became a mantra to myself in the wee hours of the night or during my bouts of crying and desperation for the loss of someone so dear to me. This was my sacred plea to make it all go away. I wasn't ready to deal with such a loss. No one had prepared me for something like this to happen. I sure didn't see it coming.

As this loss began to sink in, I couldn't possibly see all that God had in store for me from this life changing event. I never in a million years would have guessed that it would lead me to finding myself and living life more intentionally. These gifts of experiencing death were hidden under layers of mourning. I was able to eventually see that our greatest teachers, our truest gifts and our biggest blessings are disguised as our greatest losses. You can't take away the loss, but you can choose to become a better person because of it.

It goes without saying that I'll never stop missing my dad and I'll never feel completely at peace that we didn't have more time together, but I'm going to make sure his life had an impact on the way I live mine. All anyone can do is try their best to be a better person despite the tragedies in our lives.

When I mentioned the experience of death being a blessing or a gift that doesn't mean we're happy it happened. Quite frankly it's the exact opposite. I'm not happy life dealt my family this tough break, but the blessing comes in the way I chose to integrate this loss into my life. I chose for it to make me more grateful for what I do have when I have it; to stop fear in its tracks and live my life fully, for the soul searching it forced upon me at a young age and for the courage and strength I had to conjure up from the depths of my being to become the person I wanted to be. A few years after my dad passed, I went and sat on his grave, on the day I decided to give my life over to Jesus and get baptized. I thanked him that day. I thanked my dad for giving up his life to save mine. That's what it feels like to me. Through his loss I found who I really am. I found God. I look at his passing as my teacher. And I have used it repeatedly. In moments where I don't have any more to give, or when I want to give up and not stay the course I think of him and I keep going. When I want to give up on my dreams, my dad saves me again. He helps me to remember life is short so I better chase it, run with it, allow it to show me the way and enjoy every last drop.

Before losing my dad, I had experienced a close death, nine years earlier when my beloved Grandma Alice passed away, which left its own mark on my life. Losing my dad felt unique as each person we lose does. The untimely shock of it left me reeling. My dad's passing was out of nowhere, hitting me like an 18-wheeler, coming at me full speed. Instantly I felt it must have been a mistake, which left me plummeting even further into the depths of confusion and grief, being sure that God had unintentionally taken him away from us.

Although the pain has dulled from those initial days, I sure didn't think that one day, my dad's passing would be my biggest inspiration to live. I wasn't fully introduced to myself until my life had been shaken awake. God has chosen to show me so many important lessons through the tragedies in my life, but I had to be a willing participant to make that possible. With each loss, I have become a new version of myself. New doesn't always mean better. The better part is up to us.

I want you to know with certainty that if you are reading this book there is a reason. Most likely you have experienced a deep loss yourself. Maybe you are trying to wrap your head around why this happened to your loved one and thereby happened to you. You may feel hopeless, angry, deeply saddened or so low that you don't think you can ever get back to who you were before the loss took place. The truth is you won't. You will never be the same, but it will be your choice if you will become better because of it, more instead of less. Your life has forever changed and it will be up to you to accept this has happened. It will take time and you can reach out to others for support.

During the moments of complete and utter despair your grief will play tricks on you. During these difficult times, it is very important to remember that you are not alone. There are people all around you who want to support you in your grief. Reach out to them for help along the way. We are not alone in life whether we feel like we are at times or not. There is always a helping hand along the way.

Sometimes the help we are searching for may come from people who we would least expect. It's not always the ones we think it should be. Instead of finding solace in family and friends you may find it in a co-worker, a pastor, a counselor or a dedicated grief group. It's important to get out there and get the help you need. If you don't open up about what it is you need from others no one will be able to help you. It's never too late to heal.

> *"Pay attention, then, to how you spend your time. You have nothing more precious than time. In one tiny moment of time, heaven may be gained or lost."*
> -The Cloud of Unknowing

Growing up as a child I was lucky to be surrounded by family who were close. It felt almost like I was living in a world where hurt didn't exist. Or maybe I wanted to believe in the magic of life so much that I created this world for myself to live in. One where everything always worked out, there was always something special and fun to look forward to and where time stood still. In my mind, if only time would stand still I wouldn't have to lose the people I loved most, or deal with making difficult decisions, or changing so much that there were times where I didn't know who I was anymore. I wanted to live in a world where nothing bad ever happened especially not to me or the ones I loved. But eventually we each find out that this kind of world just doesn't exist at least not here on Earth.

If we are wise enough and look at life deeply enough we realize that the tragedies in life are the very thing that can save us; make us more supple, more vulnerable, more loving and more compassionate. The downturns can help to make us live more life and experience more closeness with the One who created us. I'm not saying to ask for the hard things in life to grow, I'm saying that the hard things will be given to each of us whether we like it or not. Those hard things can either take us further away from our true nature or they can compel us to dig deeper into creating the life we find most meaningful.

This book is meant to uplift, heal and inspire you to look at the tragedies in your own life as gifts that you can open at any time. The gift is in the opportunity to question why it is you are here, your ability to find your beliefs and ultimately find your way home. I'm not going to pretend I have it all figured out, but one thing is for sure I haven't stepped back from going down my path even when I was scared to death, even when I felt strong grief and suffering from the inside out, even when I beat myself up for making what I felt like were huge mistakes because each one of those disasters turned into a miracle eventually. It might not have looked like it at the time and it sure didn't always feel like it, but at some pivotal moment in my own journey I somehow decided to turn the bad into the good. You can too. We all can.

There were times on that journey that I knew down to my soul that it would require making that choice again and again. That we can give up or we can keep on going, but the choice is always up to us. I encourage you to keep on going. Never stop. Never give up. Take a break if you must, heal your heart, tend to your soul, but don't give up.

In that jarring moment when I heard of the news that my dad was gone, my life changed forever. I had never felt heartbreak like this before. The aching that surrounds the death of a loved one is immeasurable and the sting makes it feel like it will never go away. And that's just the tip of the iceberg. Not only my life but the lives of my entire family were changed and rearranged from that moment forward.

So began my journey through the most difficult year of my life. The grief I experienced was so deep. However, seven years later I am able to look back and see that this experience was meant to change my life. It wasn't by accident that this had the impact it did. However, I didn't know that eventually the loss was going to bring me a renewed sense of life and all the possibilities that exist to live a meaningful life.

I have come to a firm belief that all the things that are thrown our way are meant to be our greatest teachers and if we are able to look at our lives as this beautiful adventure of loss, pain, joy, hope and beauty we are able to experience all our lowest of lows in a manner that allows us to be capitulated far beyond anywhere we ever imagined we would go bringing us to our highest of highs. When we are able to experience life, not just think about life, but really experience it and allow it to shape us into the person we were always meant to become we open ourselves up to so much joy and freedom. Only when we are able to accept life for what it is, we are able to meander through the pain of endings we never wanted to experience, to help us live in the present moment with that much more understanding.

When I was guided to write this book to support others in their own grief I understood another's loss is just as much as a defining moment in their life as it has been in mine. Death and grief are still a taboo topic in our society and it's such a shame. We are only able to help others heal through the sharing of our hearts and our stories of loss. We should never feel like we must walk this difficult path alone. Through the loss of my dad I was able to eventually see a flicker of light at the end of the tunnel and I promised myself that my dad's passing would be for something. It had to have been for a reason and if nothing else I was going to make sure to live the life I had always wanted to live as a way to honor him. This included being more courageous and less fearful.

Each person's journey through grief will be different. We are all different so it makes sense that we will not experience it in the same way. Soon after my dad's passing I came to realize that there were two groups of people. One that was open to discussing death and one that tried to ignore it at all costs. I didn't take either of these approaches personally as it became clear to me that it's a topic many Americans are uncomfortable talking about. It's hard to bring up a subject that we are all so afraid of for ourselves and those that we love. I know it was my worst nightmare, from the time I was a young girl I was afraid of losing someone that I loved dearly. As you can imagine when it happened I literally had no other choice, but to face my biggest fear.

For quite some time after my dad's death, I would cry constantly when I wasn't around other people. I never knew you could feel so raw and hopeless. The horrible yearning I felt just to see my dad again didn't subside for a considerable amount of time. Although people around me tried to be supportive the truth was their lives moved on and soon no one mentioned it anymore.

This makes it even more important to continue grieving and not to do so in silence. It's so critical to find a support group or get help outside of your day to day life from people who understand the deep impact death has caused in your life. If we never allow ourselves to go to the deepest darkest places with our own souls we will never experience all the elements of life. Many of us want life to be lived only in the good times of life, but the reality is we must each grow. Although it's painful at best, part of growth is done in the hard times. The darkness can be a scary place to be, but as long as you don't get stuck there beyond the point you should then you can look back on this time in your life with a measure of gratitude that it helped you to learn.

A grieving heart must be emptied.

Losing my dad initially taught me what heartbreak is, but as I began to look deeper the truth bubbled up. It was much deeper than a heartbreak, it was something I refer to as a heartshatter. A heartbreak is easier to get over, it hurts, but you get on with life similarly to the way you did before the heartbreak occurred. A heartshatter is much different. It shatters everything you thought you knew about life. Your heart shatters into tiny pieces that only you can put back together the way in which you see fit. It's as if the very foundation you've been walking upon gives away underneath you and crumbles your existence.

This occurs at the same time you're experiencing a soul shift. Your soul is aligning itself with a new reality. When this occurs, it creates a significant shift in perception and is born out of a significant loss. If you've ever wondered why one loss brings about a change so severe, whereas another we accept easier, this is why. Sometimes it's caused by the losses we are not ready for or expecting. Other times it's caused by losing the ones we loved the most and the level of impact they had on our lives.

There was no manual or guidebook I was born with that told me that when I was at the young age of twenty-nine that my dad would suddenly be gone and I would have to figure out life going forward on my own without the person who created me and helped guide me. What was given to me during that time was an emptiness, a deep dark yearning to be complete again, to feel whole again. What remained was complete emptiness and in that moment, I think on some level I knew I was the only one who was going to be able to put my life back together.

To do so authentically I was going to need to do it in my own time, in my own way. This was the day my truest journey began. The day I awakened to the fact that life is short and I had work to do while I was here. Finding myself was my life's call.

As I said before, up until this loss I thought I understood what it meant when people said they were "heartbroken" over something. I soon learned that heartbreak just didn't convey what I was up against. Heartbreak insinuates that somehow you can pick up the pieces, you can keep living life the same way you did before the break happened, you can heal and put yourself back together the way you were before. My innocence was forever lost. With my heartshatter, there were pieces so far gone I wasn't sure if they were even mine any longer. The pieces of my life were so tiny and all over the place. There was no way that I was going to be able to put myself back together as I was before the shatter. I was going to have to reexamine every piece that had shattered so that I could decide what I wanted to throw away and what should come with me. I had to decide who I was now because I surely wasn't who I was before.

Looking back, I had no clue that this heartshatter would be the very thing that allowed me to find my true self. That there was a gift lurking below the pain and sorrow, something beautiful wanting to emerge, a depth to myself that I hadn't yet been introduced to. I didn't know at the time it would mean that I would be divorced in a year, that I would get so tired of carrying the weight of the world on my shoulders that I would do anything in my power to feel freedom from different vantage points, that some of my biggest dreams would come true as if by some magic fairy dust the Universe was sprinkling on me. I didn't know that I would move away from home only to finally accept myself and move back a short time later. I didn't know that I would go through one of my toughest times through the dreaded dark night of the soul and that I would come out the other side with my faith intact. None of this would have happened had the shatter not occurred. If we are lucky the shatter will happen to us all at some point in our earthly life. Navigating our way through this experience, tumultuous as it is at times, can leave us feeling raw, but somehow more alive than ever.

I knew as I sat down to write about grief it would be the topic that drew itself to me the most. When this book was only a thought in my head I imagined the entire book would be about grief, but then I realized my take on grief is one of letting it reshape you into a braver, stronger, more alive version of yourself. It was in that realization that I knew my book wasn't only about dying it was about living. That's the legacy I choose to leave behind. It's about living through the various types of deaths we endure while being fully present to them. Naturally the other piece of this book is about death. It's one I've always felt comfortable talking about and sitting with others on their journey through the trials of losing someone they love. As a Grief Share co-facilitator at my church a few years after my dad passed away it was truly an honor to sit with others who were on a similar path I had been down. It's a purpose I have been drawn to from the time my beloved Grandma Alice passed away when I was twenty years old. She is one of my greatest loves, knowing that I would not be the woman I am today without having her in my life. Maybe understanding death began to call to me after losing her because I wanted to know where she went and how I would be able to find her when my time came. More than that it began my knowing that she is still with me in a spirit form.

I've seen people around me struggle with death when it knocked on their door. The biggest struggle I uncovered that people were wrestling with was around where their loved ones went and the fear that they would never see them again. Death it seemed meant the end for so many, however, for me death meant a different way of them living right beside me. I would see people lose someone and how uncomfortable it made others to talk about it with them, let alone acknowledging it in passing, and I felt like it was such a shame that our society hasn't been taught how to handle a grieving person. Sometimes all we need is for someone to tell us how sorry they are for our loss and that they will be praying for us. Or to give us a hug and allow us to open up and cry right in front of them without a bat of an eyelash. Comforting a grieving person is an honor knowing the small gestures make a difference.

This feeling only intensified after my own dad's passing. But now I not only saw it on the grieving persons side I felt it again myself. There were so many people who didn't know how to address my grief although they knew it was there. They could see it, even feel it I'm sure. I was in pain. My life had changed forever and I hadn't wanted it to.

There were times when seeing people around me going about life as normal stung deeply. I remember people engaging me in conversations about where they were going on vacation or what their family was up to and it would cause deep emotions in me wanting to tell them I couldn't talk about any of that anymore, my dad was gone and I didn't care about anything else. I knew in my grief-stricken pain I was much more sensitive and no one meant any harm by their comments. I just had this feeling inside that I wanted to scream out that I was not okay and was in no mood to talk about a vacation or any other normal topic of conversation. Cry, get angry, or vent if you need to. This allows your grief and pain to escape through the corners of your eyes or the volume of your cry. When I noticed I was taking my dad's loss very hard, I couldn't help but think, it's okay, it just means his life was that important to me and the love I had for him was real.

What we label as grief felt somehow smaller than what I was experiencing. There was something deeper going on within me. The pain I was feeling was ripping my heart open and replacing the broken pieces with something new. Making me someone I would have to learn how to become. Grief is an interesting thing. None of us want to go through it. We'd rather avoid all the strong emotions that come along with it. If we are lucky it will reshape us into someone softer, stronger, compassionate and understanding. It's something we don't want to go through yet sometimes it is the exact thing we need to set us on a new uncharted course.

I was beside myself with profound sorrow yet I managed to get up every day and try to find the meaning in life again. The life I had known before had been ripped apart. Some of the most spiritual moments of my life stemmed from losing my dad, whom I adored, relied on and assumed would always be by my side. I wasn't equipped to handle losing what felt like an extension of myself. Who would I be without my dad to talk to, guide me and most of all love me like no one else ever would? A father's love is like no other. I wasn't sure I wanted to walk that road and couldn't imagine a future without my dad in it. All the normal thoughts began to pop in my head and they were unrelenting. Over and over I heard in my own thoughts, "my dad is gone", "I'm never going to see my dad again", or in my opinion the worst one yet, "this was a mistake."

That last one lingered for a long time causing me to believe there was something I could have done to change the outcome. These thoughts left an echo in my head that was overwhelming at best. But even deeper was this curiosity inside of me. I began to ask myself what do I believe in? What was my life all about? If my life was over instead of my dad's would I have ever really lived? This would become a theme over the next few years of my life, one I began to get answers to soon after my dad's passing.

There are so many hard things to go through after losing someone you love. Although your loss is completely out of your control, and is hard to grapple with, you can turn it into the biggest learning lesson of your life. During times of my own grief I learned very early on that I was going to feel bad as long as I allowed myself to.

After losing my dad, I lived in that grief for a year until one day I suddenly snapped out of it. I had been walking around like a sad mess of a person, unable to be alive, because my loved one no longer was. I wasn't enjoying the sheer gift of being alive and I continued to struggle through my grief.

One of the things I learned in that first year is that grief has a life of its own and everyone is going to grieve differently. I learned quickly that the size of my grief was an extension of the size of my love. And it wasn't going anywhere any time soon. It's important to be patient, loving and kind to yourself during those dark moments. When the fog doesn't seem to want to lift it is hard to think it's possible, but it will lift in time. Remember this too shall pass. The pain will dull and slowly you'll feel more and more like yourself again.

Throughout the rest of my book, there will be stories of hope and faith demonstrated. Please walk along this journey with me as I share my story with you in hopes that my experiences will be a beacon of light to you during your difficult days. You will get through it. You will live again. You will feel again and you will be an even more compassionate, kind and loving person because of your experience of loss. Keep in mind the loss of my dad has been the fuel for my inner flame not being burned out, persevering through every storm I've found myself in. My dad's passing is my why. It's why I do grief work, it's why I'm writing this book, it's why I jumped out of a plane, it's why I crossed the New York City marathon finish line, it's why I picked my entire life up and moved to Colorado on my own and it's why I keep pushing myself towards listening to my inner guidance of what to do next.

What's your why?

Chapter Two

Cracked Wide Open

"She's stuck between who she is, who she wants to be and who she should be."
- Author Unknown

After I got through the initial shock that life as I knew it was over I had to begin to accept that this was my new normal. The truth was my life would never be the same again. The thing about grief is that it can kick us where it hurts and hold us down for as long as we allow it. But there are very real stages of grief that most of us must travel through before we can see the light of day again. When we are flung into a situation that we have no idea how to handle we have two choices. We can let the grief of our situation stunt our growth and dwell in our pain to the point where we become addicted to it, or we can at some point, when the time is right, walk through the darkness knowing that our spirit will survive and even thrive for all the richness and depth of lessons we will gain from having such a raw experience.

I felt myself becoming more alive as time went on, not less. My own unique grief forced me to examine my life and where I was headed. I asked myself if I liked the outcome I saw in front of me if I stayed the course. This question forced me to get real with myself in a way that I hadn't allowed myself to do until now. I grew stronger in what I wanted out of life and what I expected of myself and those who were most integral in my life at that time. It wasn't easy to look in the mirror and question everything I had going on in my life and whether it was serving me. The relationship

I was in, the work I was doing, how I was spending my time, but really it was pointing to something so much deeper.

I had buried some of my deepest passions. I'd given up. I was twenty-nine years old and I'd given up on having the life I knew was out there for me. The one that would make me the happiest. How could that have happened to someone who was so full of life and had always yearned from some place deep down inside of herself to give something unique to the world? As I slowly, but consistently began to look at how I really felt about myself and what I wanted, I became saddened that I was holding myself back in ways that were suffocating and killing the very essence of who I was, and what I was meant to do with my life. I was becoming more aware by the day that I wasn't honoring myself in the choices I was making for my life. I was working late most evenings focusing on my work instead of having balance in all areas of my life. I finally came to realize that I was in control of my choices and that I had a say in how I spent my time. I began to see all the times in my past when I held myself back in my life from really going for it. Suddenly the dreaded four-letter word kept popping up.

F-E-A-R.

Fear of trying. Because the world teaches us, what if you try and then you fall? As if by divine intervention I began to realize a life without trying is no life lived at all. I began to believe in myself and saw that those around me could use a little encouragement, too. When I encouraged others I felt more encouraged. I was believing in myself for maybe the first time in my life and had this deep wisdom knowing that I was capable of way more than who I had become. It wasn't in a negative, being hard on myself kind of way, more of an understanding that I could really go for my dreams and achieve them.

I recognized that I had been carrying around limiting beliefs about my dreams. Believe them to be achievable for someone else, but not for me and that didn't sit well with me. I believed that the things I wanted to do were for more creative or talented folks. I was ready to set that belief down.

Honestly, how often do we shackle ourselves to limiting beliefs about what's possible in our lives? We need to challenge those thoughts with new thoughts. Train ourselves to think up new stories and new solutions to our same old patterns of thinking. We set ourselves up for hurt and regret by not being who we really are, or as big as we are capable of being. Playing small never changed anyone's life for the better. Just think of all the people who have contributed to our world by standing up and being who they came here to be. We chain ourselves to the expectations of others instead of releasing who we really are to the world. I found that I cared too much about what others thought about me and my life. My loyalty to others was proving to be detrimental to following my authentic path and I was going to have to learn to disappoint or disrupt other people's lives to save my own.

This was an area I wasn't so good at. Once I committed to something I would stay for the long haul even when it was clear things weren't working anymore. The thought of letting someone down or even worse causing hurt or pain left me stuck, motionless and unable to move forward. We tend to identify ourselves with what we do and limit ourselves by not thinking we are capable of more. I thought, since I worked in an office and got my degree in Human Resources, that was all there was for my life. I was determined to become an expert in the field and make my life fit around it. I figured this is what I had to offer and doing anything more creative wasn't a solid choice for my future. I wrongly assumed the things that lit me up and made me happy, joyful and free right down to my soul weren't the things I could make a living at, so I made an internal decision, without being conscious of it, to not follow my dreams.

On top of realizing there was more in life that I wanted to accomplish outside of the eight to five grind, I was becoming keenly aware of the direction my relationship was headed. I married my high school sweetheart, at the young age of twenty-one, well before I understood life and all that it had to offer me. I didn't fully understand what being a good partner meant. I grew up in a small town where this was the normal thing to do. More often than not, women in my family got married young and stayed in the same small town I grew up in to raise their own family. I followed the same path.

My husband and I went through a lot together and in the end, grew in separate directions. We both had good intentions and wanted it to work, but life happens. Things fall apart and we get to a place where we must choose. When we are shown two paths and can't choose both we must do the best we can with the choices we have. In the end, I chose the path less traveled. The path where I would be forced to get to know myself, learn who I am and strive to reach my fullest potential. The path I had always secretly wanted. The one where I would have to rely on myself, see what I was made of and take ownership for my life. This seemed like the most interesting path and the one that I craved the most. Ultimately, I did take that path and with it became single for the first time in my adult life, but only after a lot of anguish and indecision. I wanted to know myself so desperately that it felt like the only choice I had. The one that would lead me to myself.

A mere year after my dad's passing I couldn't shake the feeling that if I stayed on the path I was currently walking on, which included my marriage, it wouldn't end well for me. I would end up depressed, full of regret and immobile. It became much more about me and much less about how my marriage wasn't working out. I knew I wouldn't find who I was, and live the life I longed for during the wee hours of the night, when there was nothing else to distract me from myself. I had to choose myself. In doing so I chose to end my marriage at the age of thirty, after fourteen years together. With this end came a new beginning towards finding who I always knew I was. Make no mistake it wasn't easy. It came with a lot of lonely nights, doubt, uncertainty and fear of the unknown, but each day I kept going, and it kept getting easier.

I never gave up on myself and believed that if I kept going something magnificent was about to unfold. I knew that one day, not too far down the road, I was going to be able to say, I chose the rocky road, but it was the most abundant. The shakiest ground is often the most fertile. It's where we grow, expand, and awaken to our own passions, our own beliefs, our own aliveness. There was nothing alive about staying in something that ran its course. There was something brazen and bold about admitting to not only myself, but the entire world that my marriage simply was not working for me anymore. The message I was sending to the Universe was that I finally loved myself enough to do something for me.

Once I made this decision I couldn't' believe the women who came out of the woodwork telling me they wish they could do what I had just done. They had varying degrees of why they thought they couldn't make it on their own. I could clearly see our beliefs about ourselves affect how we live our lives. It's in changing our beliefs that we have the power to change our lives. The truth was there was nothing different about me that made me able to move on with my life other than I stayed strong, and even when I had weak moments, I used those moments to help build my willpower and strength. I had come this far with my decision to be single for the first time in my adult life and now there was no chance I was going to wipe away all my internal work just to turn around to go back where I'd always been. I couldn't risk not knowing the woman I would become. It was too late to turn around. I had made a promise to myself. I vowed to know my own soul and that meant I was going to have to stay committed and do the work it would take to release my potential.

Stepping out on my own felt freeing. I had never just had myself to take care of before and I began learning an entirely new skillset. I evaluated how I was spending my time and began implementing some of my favorite activities like yoga, working out, going on long bike rides and writing into my weekly routine. Doing the things, I enjoyed lifted my spirits and gave me a sense of fulfillment. I would write goals on little post-it notes around my apartment. When I would find them months later I would be astonished that I had checked each goal off my list without even being focused on it. Life was going smoother than it ever had. There was an easy flow to my life that I wasn't accustomed to. I found that while it was nice to be in a partnership there was something really lovely about being at a place in my life where I was focused solely on myself and being in a healthy, balanced place for no one other than me. Being alone also made me keenly aware that I was responsible for my own life, my own happiness, my own choices and how the story of my life turned out. It was all my making. I finally felt like I could breathe for the first time since my dad's passing a year before. I began to take time to do the things I'd always wanted to do.

There were times I had to get real with myself and ask why my relationship didn't work out after spending so many years together. The answers I came up with were pretty astounding and some of them I wasn't very proud of. I didn't like that my expectations were sometimes unreasonable and unfair, that I blamed some of my unhappiness on him or the biggest reason in my mind was that I simply committed to something at such a young age that I didn't fully understand. I was careful not to put blame on either party, to come at it from a place of learning and growth, instead of a place of regret or anger.

I'll never forget the moment I decided to leave. I looked in the mirror, into my own eyes, into my own being and realized for maybe the first time in a long time that I loved the woman staring back at me. I loved her heart, her compassion, her sweetness and now it was time to take care of her. If I didn't leave now my life would never change and I would never become who I wanted to be. It wasn't about anyone else at that point. Not even about my husband. It was about me taking care of me. Taking care of the beautiful soul that was right in front of me, screaming out for help, telling me in her eyes that things weren't okay and there was no end in sight unless something got rearranged. After all, God put this soul inside of my body to take care of, no one else's. So much had happened in the year prior to this reckoning. So much pain and suffering from losing my dad and then on top of it my marriage just wasn't working and that girl in front of me in the mirror just simply had had enough. It was time to push taking care of everyone else to the side and start taking care of her. Most importantly she was begging to find the spark again, the spark in her own eye.

So, I did something brave, something I hadn't ever done. I listened to those eyes looking back at me, I listened to the voice screaming inside telling me it was time to go, it was time to live, it was time to honor her. Instead of continuing to stuff all her dreams deep down inside until they were barely visible all in the name of making others happy. She wanted her adventure. It was time to not make her wrong for feeling what she felt, to not make her out to be a villain just because she wanted something different.

Listen I did. Listening in a non-judgmental, loving tone, changed everything. I saw that there was no right or wrong person in this situation. There was no angel and no devil. There was no bad person and no good person. There were just two people who needed to go their separate ways. I was done pretending that things were okay. As I thought back and considered the last year of my life I had a deep understanding and appreciation that if my dad had not passed I wouldn't have had the strength to do what I was about to do. Sometimes we must go through what we think is the worst possible thing in order to see that we have the strength to endure. Those difficult, trying times in life prepare us for some of our greatest transformations, which ultimately lead to our biggest transitions. They set us on the path we are meant to take. The shaking up of our lives provides us with the opportunity to begin again. I knew I would survive the loss of my marriage because I had survived the loss of my dad and if either of those were going to break me it would not be this one.

As free as I felt, I wanted the same feeling for my ex-husband. My love for him as a person, as a friend and as someone who stood by me through a lot of life didn't end just because my address changed. I wanted better for him and to love and be loved in the way he deserved. And somewhere in my heart, I had to admit that he deserved a better fit for his life, too. This gave me profound comfort knowing in my heart that this was the best decision. I found out through the loss of my dad that life is painfully short and by golly I was going to live it even if I had to clear some internal junk to get there. I was no longer afraid to do the work. I was excited to see who I was without any other distraction outside of myself. I've never been afraid of a challenge and so I began to look forward, to thrive from the challenges I decided to take on, the ones that were important to me, the ones that resonated with my very being.

I'll never forget the spring day that I moved out on my own. There was a feeling in the air that I was on the right path for my life. That I was moving towards what I wanted to learn in this lifetime. Yes, I had the typical guilt associated with making a major life change and hurting someone I loved, but in the end we got through it. We remain friends and I'd like to think we are both better people because of our time together and the lessons we learned from the years we spent together.

Now here I was on my own to find my way. I was fast becoming the woman I had always longed to be. Instead of just talking about the things I wanted to do in life I began living them, experiencing them, eating them up.

When my dad passed away, I was training for my first half marathon. Although I had never run more than four miles at one time I had always dreamed of running in a race. One day while surfing the internet I came across a news article discussing the results of the New York City Marathon. There was something that clicked in me that said you want to do that someday. At that point in my life, it seemed far fetched, as I was lying in bed reading the story of the runners who trained and overcame obstacles to cross the finish line. I wasn't a runner, I never had been. I barely had time to work out as it was. I was married at the time and between working a full-time job well into the evenings on most days and spending time with family it was a long shot that I would run in a marathon. I had another one of those dreaded feelings in the pit of my stomach, the one that crops up and tells you that you're not going to do the thing you really want to do. I was downright sick of the resignation that welled up inside of me so easily.

Instead of listening to that fear and making it real, I figured I had to start somewhere. When I heard about some co-workers training for a local half marathon in Lincoln, Nebraska, I figured it was as good a time as any to put myself out there. The year before my dad had passed, I started to train for what I thought would be my first half marathon, but before I could get very many runs under my belt my dad had passed. When training rolled around the following year I figured it was time to recommit and try again. This time I would do it not only for myself, but for my dad. I promised myself that losing him would be for something. If the only reason I could come up with was to push me to live my life differently it would have to mean at least one life was changed.

With that thought in mind, I signed up and set out to run the half marathon for the second time. I'll never forget my first night of training.

It was a frigid January evening like most winter evenings in Nebraska. I had been living on my own now for about nine months and it took all my motivation to leave my cozy, warm little apartment, to trudge my way through the snow to the work out room. I reluctantly got on the treadmill and pressed the start button. But something changed just as I took my first step. I made the decision that I was going to do this. It didn't matter that I had never ran before. It didn't matter that I might not end up being the fastest runner or even close to it. It didn't matter that until this very day at thirty-one years old I hadn't run more than four miles at any one time.

I learned that every journey starts with one step and so I proceeded to fight for that first mile. I fought to prove something to that voice inside of myself that had so easily talked me out of things in the past. I fought to make that voice wrong and my heart right. We all have the power to make new choices, live new lives and be the person that makes us feel the best about ourselves. I also knew after that first mile that it wouldn't be easy. I would have to be diligent and start changing the way I thought about my ability to succeed. I would have to start believing I could achieve new goals and that I would be able to accomplish things I'd never done before. I would have to be positive, even when I wanted to give up. I quickly learned that running is a mental game. Your mind and body often want to fail you, but your spirit is so much bigger than either of these. My spirit would soar each time I finished a run. I began to look forward to the time of day when I could just go outside and run. It became my sanctuary, my great escape and freed me from my own personal prison of doubt and worry. It was my stress reliever and my time to spend in prayer. My moving meditation.

The greatest battle of our lives is the one with ourselves. I took that battle head-on and ended up running my first half marathon a mere four months later. I'll never forget the anticipation and nervousness I had standing behind the starting line in the early morning of May 2012, when I set out to run my first race. The ten thousand plus runners surrounding me looked like pros and I was filled with excitement to experience this moment. I couldn't believe it when I had already gone eight miles without much of a glitch. Then there was the slow steady hill. I climbed my way to the top not daring to look backward, only forward. There was nothing like crossing the finish line on the football field at University of Nebraska at Lincoln and seeing yourself on the big screen. I could hardly believe that I had ran the entire 13.1 miles without stopping to walk once. To finish that run and collapse into the arms of family and friends meant the world to me. My brother and sister-in-law being there to cheer me on was the cherry on top of the cake. They would be there to greet me at many of my other runs and mini triathlons I would embark upon over the next few years. Knowing they were there cheering me along with my cousin Tony and friend Janette always kept me going even when my mind wanted to tell me different. That was the day I felt like a true runner. It taught me that anything we put our minds to really is possible. We can go the distance by taking one small, but mighty step at a time.

As I was making these changes in my life, I'd feel that old familiar friend come back again. The one who was much wiser than myself. The one who promised there was more to unearth and discover about who I really was. The one that would require a lot of bravery on my part.

A lot of people who go through separation and divorce get caught up in thinking they are leaving because the other person just isn't cutting it. After some time and reflection, I realized leaving my marriage was more about me than it was about anyone else. There was something brewing in me that needed to grow and evolve.

Unfortunately, in the confines of a relationship I was not going to find what I was looking for, which was myself. Here I was facing another huge loss, barely over the age of thirty. It hit me that I'd have more grief, more darkness to walk through with this divorce. But something magical happened. Maybe it happened because it was the right thing to do, but the extreme grief I experienced with the loss of my dad never came with the divorce. Maybe it was because I was strong enough to handle the breakup of my fourteen-year relationship after going through the trauma of losing my dad. Maybe the loss of my dad had in some ways made me stronger than I'd ever been. Not because I took the end of my marriage lightly as everything in me said that divorce just wasn't acceptable. I believed in marriage and my upbringing told me it wasn't okay to get a divorce.

Maybe what made it less difficult was we both had long futures ahead of us. Futures where we could still make a profound difference in the world in our own way. Or maybe yet, it was because after losing my dad and now my marriage I had the strongest urge I'd ever had to experience living and a new beginning after all the endings that had surrounded me.

I longed to live despite all the damage that had been done in my life recently. I'd already experienced my worst nightmare of losing someone I loved dearly, it left me feeling like I could handle walking the road of divorce, which says a lot with growing up in a family where marriage was valued and you stuck it out. Here I was walking the road less traveled and was single for the first time since I was a teenager in high school when my ex-husband and I first started dating. Here I was almost fifteen years later, wondering if I wasted parts of both of our lives, but knowing in my heart it was time well spent.

Having felt like I failed at marriage, which I believe is meant to be one of the greatest gifts of life felt heavy. We are so incredibly hard on ourselves when things don't work out. Reliving all the moments I could have made different choices or the things I could have done to have a different ending made me feel even worse. I found myself pondering the question, why do we look at endings as failures when there is always success in simply trying?

The relationship had simply served its purpose and it was time to move on. I was able to reconcile that this specific relationship gave me so much learning about myself, who I am, what I'm willing to live with and who I longed to be in the future. I wouldn't have gotten those lessons in the way I did if I hadn't been married.

I was ready to find the woman that lived inside of me and break the glass case she'd been confined to all of these years. I wanted her to experience life on her terms and to finally be free. Free from pain, guilt, shame and self-loathing, never trusting herself to make the big decisions in life. Now was her time. As I packed my last bag and left a house that had been my home for what would be the final time, I understood the road would be long and wind in directions I probably wouldn't always want to go, but I also knew deep down that I was embarking on my truest journey. The one I was sent here to take.

I never would have guessed by leaving a situation that no longer worked for my soul I was opening a myriad of doors I would sometimes walk through confidently and others I would be pulled through looking back later wondering if I was in my right mind. The truth is I felt more alive not knowing what was coming next than when it was all mapped out for me. As if I was an actor in a play I wasn't sure I wanted to be in. What do we do when we want to rewrite the script? We must be strong, get up our gumption and do what we need to do. Sometimes that involves hurting those we've loved the most.

As a society, we get caught up in things lasting forever. We look at it as failure when they don't go the distance; instead of honoring our journeys and understanding that some things only last for the time they are meant to. Some relationships just aren't meant to go the distance. Once they serve their purpose, it is just as honoring to let the situation be set free, to move on with dignity and respect for everyone involved. Why would we want to cage a wild horse? We wouldn't. Yet we have no problem caging ourselves to a situation that no longer feeds us spiritually, emotionally, physically or otherwise.

I've found the best relationships I've experienced have an understanding that the Universe put us together for a reason and that there may be a timetable to that reason. One that no amount of begging, pleading or groveling will change. We must trust that if they are meant to stay they will. There's great comfort in knowing that there's really nothing you can do to disrupt the Universe's plan for those that are meant to be in your life. The Universe will remove them just as suddenly as it brings them. For those that are meant to stay there is no amount of anything you can do to keep them away, just as there is nothing you can do to keep those who are meant to go. We cannot chain another's soul to our own. God won't allow it. When there is a plan there is a plan and you can do nothing to disrupt it from happening. It might take you longer, you might go off your path, but you will just as suddenly be forced back upon it. We can either accept this or fight against it. It's up to us the amount of suffering we are willing to endure. Do we choose to make life easier or harder?

There have been times on my journey where I am sure God was trying to bop me upside the head to get my attention and I was too stubborn to listen. I wanted to be right, I wanted things that weren't working to work. When I feel the most peace in my life is when I surrender to the plan and accept impermanence as one of my greatest teachers. Then I can be at peace, if only for a moment. As one of my favorite poems says, relationships are meant for a reason, a season or a lifetime and we should cherish them all equally.

Reason, Season, Lifetime
By Unknown Author

People come into your life for a reason, a season or a lifetime.
When you figure out which one it is, you will
know what to do for each person.
When someone is in your life for a reason, it is
usually to meet a need you have expressed.
Some people come into your life for a season, because
your turn has come to share, grow or learn.
Lifetime relationships teach you lifetime lessons; things you must
build upon in order to have a solid emotional foundation.
Your job is to accept the lesson, love the person, and put what you
have learned to use in all other relationships and areas of your life.

As I dug deeper, I realized that my true nature was attachment. Our souls have seen so much, done so much, lost so much that it gives us reassurance to have the illusion that something will last forever. The truth is we are never truly in control and some things will never last forever, no matter how hard we try. We've been on our own journey for eternity and we will continue down that path as well. God is the only relationship we have forever, day in and day out. People are separated from their attachments all the time by death, divorce, loss of a job, health issues, and so on.

If you dig even deeper you'll see that this is only one lifetime. I believe that the reason we feel like we already know someone the first time we meet them is because we do. Souls recognize each other by the love they have felt before. We will be with partners at the right time in our soul's evolution. Life is about the soul's journey around the sun. Even when we come across souls that we have past karma with the relationship can start out as loving to lure us into doing our work. When we meet people and it's a difficult connection from the beginning we don't tend to go towards them, but as soon as we are drawn to something out of love we are more likely to stick with it even when the energy gets rough between us. In this lays part of the mystery and brilliance of the Universe. And if we are going to say a hearty "yes" to learning our lessons we are going to have to say "yes" to the connections that feel good and the ones that don't.

The truth is, if we are going to do what we came here to do, it's going to take some gumption on our part and a whole lot of strength and endurance to keep going. Do you even see how strong and brave you are to choose to come here? The Earth plane is not an easy place to live. The sheer fact you made your way here says something big about your bravery. You've got to believe in yourself. When you face resistance, doubt your abilities or fear what those around you think, remember you've got this! Don't be concerned with what others think of your choices. Any negative thoughts will only hold you back. We need to understand that people only try to hold others back because it triggers their own fears. We internalize things so if someone else is changing their life, what does that say about ours? That's how we think. We're not comfortable with not knowing. Let their hesitations and judgments be about them and not you. Don't ever give your power to someone else. Keep walking down your path, crawl if you must, but keep going, if only step by tiny step.

Finding people who want to hold you back is easy. There is no skill in that. Finding people who lift you up higher to reach for your dreams takes skill. There's character in those people, there's self-worth in those people. It takes skill, effort and a certain amount of self-esteem to look at another human being and see their magnificence. Those are the people you should want to surround yourself with, be with, live your life with and love. Those people know the value of their own soul and therefore won't squash yours. The ones that talk relentlessly about their fears, will be the ones who will squash your dreams. Pay them no attention. Don't make the mistake of turning their fears into your worries. We all have plenty of our own fears that we don't need to take on the fears of others; leaving our dreams in the dust in their wake. Understand that they are on a different part of their journey than you are and keep on trucking towards your happily ever after.

Remember when we change and get more committed to our path it causes other people to fear what your change is going to cause in their life. The thing I've learned about change is that it's not easy for many of us and it can come at a cost. What I mean by that is when you decide you want to change and pursue a new path it usually comes with a change to your current relationships as well. You can't change without change happening in areas of your life that other people may not want to happen. You may not look at things the same or want the same things in life that you used to want. This can be a time that's scary for you and those around you. You may be feeling a sense of renewal, dedication and purpose, but that doesn't mean those around you do. They may fear the change because if things with you are changing that may mean things will change for them, too. And they may not have signed up for the changes you want to make.

This is what happens to a lot of marriages. Two people get married at a point in time where their lives are in unison and they don't take into consideration all the variables that may change in the future. This is one of the reasons we should never go into any relationship thinking we are going to change someone to make them more of what we want them to be. Who are we to think we can change someone else and not allow the other person the freedom to be who they are? This gives us the freedom to be who we are and even more to be accepted and loved for being who we are.

After my divorce, I had to learn this the hard way. With each passing day, it became clear that the only person holding me back from the love and acceptance I craved all those years was myself. The day I recognized and then accepted that was the day I got my power back. I was indeed in charge of how I felt about myself. I truly had to learn how to love myself before another would be able to. The first shift I had with this was in January 2012. I've always loved a new year. They feel so open, free and full of possibility. This was the first January I spent as a single woman ringing it in on my own terms. The last two years had been nothing but difficult at best. I had spent over half of the previous year single, with a minor blip of dating someone who wasn't right for me or my spiritual development. Here I was on New Year's Day confronted with nothing but myself. I knew deep in my bones that I wanted more than anything to make a transformation in my life and although I didn't know how I would get there I knew I would. I decided to do something different than I've ever done to ring in this fresh crisp new year.

I took a jog outside. It was freezing cold with snow on the ground, but I didn't care. Breathing in that cold winter air helped me get clear on what I really longed for in my life. Maybe it was the fresh air going to my head or maybe it was God Himself trying to get through to me, but something clicked, something changed. I wanted more than ever to find myself. The true me. As I looked up ahead in the distance, my favorite bridge stood before me, with the most beautiful morning sun shining off to my left. I decided to stop at that bridge to pray. This was one of the first times I had prayed in a long time. I talked directly to God in a way I hadn't done before. I asked Him to help me make 2012 one of the best years of my life, to somehow help me get back on a brighter path. I realized if my dad's life hadn't been cut short I may never have fully understood that my life was speeding along all too fast. I was finally ready to get down to why I was sent here. Boy was I going to find out. Ready or not here God comes.

Little did I know 2012 would be the year I would give my life over to God, many months later running on a different trail, on a much different day.

Chapter Three

Born to Love

The Invitation
By Oriah Mountain Dreamer

It doesn't interest me what you do for a living.
I want to know what you ache for and if you dare
to dream of meeting your heart's longing.
I want to know if you will risk looking like a fool for love,
for your dream, for the adventure of being alive.
I want to know if you can sit with pain, mine or your own,
without moving to hide it, or fade it, or fix it.
I want to know if you can live with failure, yours and mine, and still stand
at the edge of the lake and shout to the silver of the full moon, "Yes."
It doesn't interest me who you know or how you came to be here. I want to
know if you will stand in the centre of the fire with me and not shrink back.
I want to know if you can be alone with yourself and if you
truly like the company you keep in the empty moments.

Another area of my life I became curious about was relationships. Within each one of us there is a craving to love and be loved in return. We all have a desire to connect, to love and be loved. I wanted to delve into past patterns and look at how I viewed relationships based on how I had seen relationships around me unfold since I was a young girl. I wanted to take this time to learn the lessons I needed to learn surrounding relationships so that I could have a successful one in the future and not repeat past mistakes and patterns. Since I never wanted to be in the same situation again I had to make sure I was strong enough within myself before I made another serious commitment. I also understood that learning comes with experience and I was going to have to open myself up to being vulnerable in the future and give someone new a chance.

It helped that I've always truly believed that the right people come along our path and every experience and person whom we encounter are there to teach us something unique along our journey. Perhaps they offer us something we came here to learn and in turn we are their teacher as well.

I became just as interested in learning about love as I was about every other area of my life. When it comes to relationships of the romantic kind we must be careful that we're not using these partnerships to fill a void we have within ourselves. If we do, we are only perpetuating a need to feel validated outside of ourselves, which creates a perfect storm. When we find a partner who we can move through life's challenges with we know we've found a relationship worth holding onto.

My single days have really challenged me to be good to myself first and foremost. This means a lot of different things and I'm not always successful at it, but as I've grown along my journey I've learned it applies to many areas of my life. The friends we keep, the way we treat and talk about our bodies, the quality of how we spend our time and the voices we allow into our own minds. Do we have positive self-speak or do we tend to get more negative in our heads? This adds up to a big difference in our life experience.

Being kind and loving really does start with how we treat ourselves. After my divorce, I began to get almost obsessed with finding the right person for me. Some place deep inside I knew that God had other plans for me. Plans for me to grow closer to Him without having a partner and soon I took on that journey with more passion than I had ever felt towards knowing anyone else in my life. I began to follow His steps, going where He guided me to go.

Sure, I had a few encounters with dating, but each one was brief, ending before it really had enough time to begin. Each heartbreak I experienced was painful to say the least, but when I would have doubts about my future including, "the love of my life", I tried my best to give it over to God and lay it at His feet realizing the only person I truly wanted was "the one" He chose for me. I learned how to pick myself up after each disappointment and keep on moving along my path. It helped that I had found some very fulfilling past times that kept my attention elsewhere. To be honest, I kept myself so busy living life that there were times I barely noticed I still hadn't found someone to share my life with. It didn't mean I wanted it any less, it just meant that I believed in God's timing even when I wasn't as patient as I hoped I would be. Plus, I promised myself after my divorce that I would never settle. I didn't want to go through all the heartache and pain I had been through just to end up with the wrong person. Somewhere deep inside I knew there were many lessons I was going to be called to learn on my own first. I was still finding out who I was and healing from the letdown of going through a very personal experience with deciding to end my marriage. I knew time alone was the best thing for me. I found myself at times pondering if I was meant to be alone forever, but somewhere inside I'd carry on and keep trusting that if God had someone for me He would make it known. After being single for several years, I remember running on the trail one day after I had asked God for several days when He was going to send me "my person." During the run, I heard the Lord speak to me saying, "When you are ready the right person will come." That gave me hope, knowing that God had a plan. It felt like a sweet promise made to me, something to look forward to when the time was right.

Once again, I was guided to look internally for my own happiness, asking myself questions like am I keeping important promises I make to myself? If the answer was yes, I knew all I must do is keep up the good work. If the answer was no, I knew I had some work to do. When we don't keep promises to ourselves, how do you expect to attract people who will keep the promises they make to us? Law of attraction says we will attract that which we put out to the Universe. If I wanted to attract the right partner who would bring me the experiences in life I desired, I had to first learn how to attract what I wanted into my own life.

Relationships are meant to teach us how to extend unconditional love to ourselves and others. The relationship we have with ourselves is the most important relationship we will ever have after our relationship with God. When you think about it, you are the only one you will go your entire lifetime with. There is no other person who will see you through every experience except for yourself. The quality of our external relationships really does mimic the quality of our internal relationship with ourselves. If being in a solid, committed, grounded, loving relationship is your ultimate goal you must first start with your relationship with yourself.

This takes just as much time, effort and commitment as it does to be in a partnership. During my single days, I have made it a priority to go on, "solo soul trips", where I go on a get-away with myself and do the things in life I love. I've learned how to fill my time with activities, hobbies, travel and spiritual quests all in the name of enjoying my own time with myself. There is nothing that I won't do on my own. I found that others would shun the idea of going to a movie on their own or taking themselves on a dinner date when they had a craving for a restaurant. Not me. There was no way I was going to miss out on a chunk of my life just because I didn't want to be seen alone. I would tell people, "I'm not alone, I'm with myself." What better way is there to spend life than to be with yourself? Why do we say we are alone when we do things on our own? Instead it really is about being with ourselves. Maybe it's that free-spirited, independent woman that lives inside of me, but I don't conform to ideas that keeps us small when we are all so much bigger than our thoughts.

Love is the most healing element on Earth.
Love will heal your heart and mend your soul.

Another lesson I learned about relationships is that it is vital to the health and wellbeing of any relationship to approach people as gifts. It changes our perspective in an instant. We can get more excited about the new purse or cell phone we just purchased than we do the old friend we ran into at the mall.

We all need more love and excitement for those around us. We don't need more hurt, more pain, more suffering, more worry, or more stress in our lives. We need more acceptance, more passion, more inspiration and more hope. It's up to each one of us to make the commitment, make the choice, make the decision to bring more of the positive energies into our relationships. This is what will help heal the world.

First, we must learn how to be that positive force in our own lives. It starts with the small moments that add up. If a stranger were standing in front of you, telling you about a hurt they are carrying, what would you tell them? The majority of us might say something like, "don't be so hard on yourself", "everything is going to be okay", or "take care of yourself." We need to learn to do that same thing for ourselves. We are our own worst critic. We are much harder on ourselves than anyone else is on us. The kindness we extend to strangers must be the kindness we give to ourselves. In my estimation the biggest problem on our planet today is that we don't take care of ourselves very well so how can we do a good job of taking care of each other? Many wake up to go to jobs we are miserable in, engage in relationships that aren't healthy for us and consume ourselves in negative thinking about our self-worth and what's possible in our lives. We need more acceptance, more genuine interest in each other's lives, and our overall well-being.

> *Our biggest dream shouldn't be in finding someone else,*
> *rather it should be in finding ourselves.*

When you learn to commit to yourself it becomes easier to commit to someone else. We all know what it feels like to be fully invested in something whether it be a relationship, a job, or a project. On the flip side, we also know what it feels like to be on the outskirts of a commitment. The latter feels much different, we are more restless, less invested and usually less happy because of it.

If you're going to finish anything to its completion it's going to take an extreme amount of patience and perseverance. Whether it be a relationship, a job, a project or the most important human accomplishment of all, extending love to others past the point you thought was possible. It's these relationships that try us, often shaking us to our core, requiring more of us that help us grow. I've found it's easy to love those who don't challenge us or make us uncomfortable in some way. Those that require more from us are true gifts along our journey to expand our way of thinking and existing in this world. To shut yourself off from the experience would mean you're not yet open to this kind of growth. These types of relationships are our mirrors. They open us up to look at the unhealed parts of ourselves to do the most difficult work we can do here. Spiritual healing and letting go. It's like an onion whose layers need to be peeled back one by one until it gets to the center where freedom lives. It's like a soul colonic. It's not only our bodies that need to be rid of waste. It's also the same for our souls.

> *"Important encounters are planned by the souls*
> *long before the bodies see each other."*
> *-Paulo Coelho*

Why do you think that certain people come across your path at a certain time? I believe it's because we are ready to learn and teach what we were brought here to gain and give the other person. Have you ever come across someone who feels so familiar to you that you have an instant recognition you've known them before? It's because you have. Souls recognize one another by the love they have felt for one another in the past. God sends us to Earth with our soul tribe who is here to teach us what we need to learn when we need to learn it.

Relationships are our biggest spiritual teacher. If you want to practice a religion or spirituality start by practicing kindness, humility and love with each relationship you have. Strive to practice the type of kindness Jesus taught and your life will be changed forever. Gratitude is another spiritual practice we can each start as a daily ritual. When we're not feeling good it's usually because we're not practicing gratitude. A significant place to start is by showing gratitude to those around us. People are the most important reason we are alive and the most life giving force we can experience.

Relationships bring with them the power to change you in ways you never thought possible merely by the experiences they bring. Sometimes we are lucky enough to cross paths with another soul, one that sets ours on fire and changes us in ways we never would have been able to, if they hadn't come into our lives. That's not meant to say that the experiences are always good ones. Difficult experiences have the power to give us the push for our soul to grow. To make us better because of them. They usually bring truth to our lives. Truth that we can't dare turn away from. In turn the transformation begins.

To handle the changing winds of life, surround yourself with people who have been where you are, and can help you navigate the choppy waters of life. It's also important to have people who are living the kind of life you would like to emulate. Be wary of taking advice from those who aren't doing such a hot job handling their own obstacles. If you look towards someone who is working through their junk in a positive, spiritually translucent way that is probably someone who you want to confide in.

You can tell a lot about a person by how they choose to handle their demons. If they go within as a means of growth and introspection they are on a path towards self-acceptance and awareness. If they tend to deal with their issues outwardly by way of searching for their own healing in another or with drugs or alcohol they may very well still be on a spiritual journey; you just might ask yourself if that is a road you will choose to go down with them. If they are still caught up in dumbing down their senses to get through life instead of cracking themselves open fully to the experience of looking within for their own answers. We are all meant to have our own experiences. What worked for them may or may not work for you.

My belief is that we should all follow our own path to lead us to our own promised land, the place that intersects with our own holy grail of life, the place within us where we humbly bow down to the sacredness of our being. Too often we get caught up in a trap of feeling like we need to travel the road our parents or friends did instead of honoring the voice within. There's no doubt there's wisdom to be gained from those around us, but not in the name of abandoning our own way of doing things. When you begin separating yourself from the opinions of those around you, you'll know you've grown beyond other people's expectations.

I've had several relationships where I found myself growing beyond them simply because of the way the person viewed our connection. They were comfortable with me relying on their advice and I no longer needed it. You'll find those relationships suddenly drift away when they aren't able to respect the new boundaries you've set in place for yourself. We recognize our own growth because we've lived it, but others don't always see it largely due to it making them uncomfortable to no longer interact with us in the same way they did before. Don't be afraid to let those relationships go, or minimize the frequency of them, they will only stunt your growth, and hold you captive to the old you. It doesn't mean you don't honor and love them. It just means you don't need the stagnant energy the relationship brings with it.

> *"Think of love like the industrious bee, gathering the sweets from every flower and depositing them in the soul of the person who loves."*
> -St. John Chrysostom

Relationships have a way of bringing up our own feelings of worthiness. Being worthy is something we are born with, it's an innate human trait. There is no one on this planet that isn't worthy of every good thing imaginable. In fact, God wants us to experience only the best that life has to offer. We get into our own heads about what we are worthy or not worthy of. One person is not more or less worthy than another. That simply doesn't exist in reality.

Once you believe that you are worthy of all good things, you will begin to allow yourself to experience them. Let's take love for example, some people have been brought up to believe that they are not worthy of love because of their past. Some may have been in situations where they were treated less than what they deserved to be treated. They may stay stuck in that line of thinking by believing they must not deserve to be loved because they have never been shown unconditional love. They may continue to perpetuate this cycle their entire lives unless they begin to think they are capable of the experience of love. No matter how much someone wants to give them love they will never be open to receive it until they themselves are open to being loved. You will not experience something in your life you are not ready for. If all you are ready to experience is lack of love that is what will continue to show up for you. You'll be perpetually caught up in relationships where the love is lacking.

As humans, we walk around putting out vibes to the world saying this is what I want to experience because this is all that I think I'm worthy of experiencing. Once you understand this you can begin to shift to putting out different vibes and therefore attracting a better life experience. Once you truly come to an inner place of worthiness and put the vibe out to the Universe of being worthy you will begin attracting a completely different quality of person into your life and different life experiences. If you are wondering what you are putting out, take a quick inventory of your relationships right now. Who are you attracting into your life? If it isn't the quality of relationship you want to be attracting, you should think about how you are showing up in your life. Are you walking around with thoughts that you are not enough or thoughts that you are enough?

You can look at this for any area of your life. If you're struggling or having a hard time attracting what it is you want to attract then you are either not clear with what you want, or you don't yet believe on an internal level that you are deserving of what you want to attract. People have changed their entire life circumstances with the thoughts they allow to go through their heads about what they think they are worthy of. We must be willing to take an honest look at our thoughts and be keenly aware of changing them to get a different outcome.

We've all heard the term fake it till you make it and there is some truth in that. Don't wait to do what you really love until you think you've made it because that day will never come. We have never truly "made it" anyhow. We always have more to learn, more to experience and more to give. We have more easy times ahead of us and more trials. It's life. It's what we signed up for and it's why we chose to make another appearance here on Earth. We have things left to learn. We tend to think love is a feeling, either you have it or you don't, but I think love is also a choice. When we choose love, we choose to stand by someone even when it's not easy, because to love another is to love yourself. Love conquers all the difficulties in life. Love is our safe harbor in the midst of the storm.

I invite you to create a movement. A movement within your own heart that you will live life to the fullest. With each day, month, year that you're given it will uncover more of the beauty you hold within. Each experience good, bad or indifferent will leave a mark so deep within yourself that gratitude pours out of you. That you become more passionate, not less, as you grow, evolve and learn. That you never forget the most important piece of the human condition, that we all crave to love and be loved. In the end love is what makes you rise each morning to the sound of your own breath, your own heartbeat, your own mortality knowing on some level that this thing we are doing - this rising, this living, this evolving - will one day cease and we will be on the other side wishing we had breathed slower, loved deeper. It's never too late to unravel the areas within yourself that lack love and begin again.

I am trying. Every. Single. Day. And the love that is freely pouring out of me today is a gift.

Chapter Four

Dream On, Moon Child

> *"Without leaps of imagination, or dreaming, we lose the excitement of possibilities. Dreaming, after all, is a form of planning."*
> -Gloria Steinem

One thing I've realized is the dreams we have might seem crazy to some, impossible to another or even farfetched to them. On the other hand, there is this entirely other group of people, the ones who light up when you talk about your passions, why you're here and what you are meant to be doing. Those are the ones who have chased after a dream themselves. We all need to hear each other's dreams because we might just spark a flame inside of someone else to unlock their hidden purpose. There is yet another group who are already living bravely so they don't even understand why we wouldn't already be taking the steps to live the life we want to live. For them living a brave life is like knowing the back of their hand, so when you bring up the fear that grips you in the middle of the night they just don't seem to relate. Maybe they've always been brave or maybe they crossed that bridge eons ago so they forget exactly what it's like to step off that cliff for maybe the first time in their lives.

Don't get caught up in watching someone else live your dreams.

Have you ever found yourself saying I wish I could do this or that or I wish I could be that courageous to follow my own path like that person is doing? Let's not get curious about the ways in which that person does it instead let's get curious about why we don't think we are courageous enough to do it. That's where the real work and potential for transformation lies. It's in our thoughts about what is possible for our lives that needs the tweaking. Be okay with not caring what anyone else thinks. It just ends up getting in the way of taking action. And that's not meant to be in a thoughtless or harsh way. You should not be concerned with what others think about what you want to do with your life.

You can always take a break, but never quit. Say "yes" to life more often than you say "no" and you'll be amazed at how your life opens to possibility. It's inevitable that there will be times where you try something and it doesn't work out. Don't let this discourage you into never trying again. It's okay to take a breather and give yourself time to recuperate, but don't let it keep you from believing in your dreams. And more importantly taking action towards them. I've become much less interested in hearing about dreams and much more interested in hearing about the action that is being taken towards the dream. Don't get me wrong, inspiration is a very useful tool, but it's what you do with that inspiration that counts. Someone once told me, "if your head stays in the clouds, your feet will land in the same spot when you come back down." That has stuck with me and made me realize we must let our inspiration move us into action. Then and only then will we find our reality transformed.

Dreams do come true, but not in the way that a lot of us may imagine. They come true through dedication and commitment to our dream. God whispers our dreams gently into our ears, but He can't come down from Heaven and do it for us. Plus, wouldn't that take away the satisfaction we feel when we do it for ourselves? I wrestled with this on and off for years, I saw a vision, one I believe God gave me for my life yet I became confused on how to get there. I would start and stop repeatedly. I would become inspired and focused, and then before any real breakthrough happened, I would become overwhelmed and discouraged time and time again. I wasn't getting the results and outcomes in life I so desperately longed for and felt stuck in the same place. Until I realized that God would clear the path for me when it was time, but I still had to do my part. This book you are reading right now was once only a dream yet I knew it would come to fruition when the time was right. Once I realized I had God's full backing and support it came easier for me to finish. We must do our part before God can do His. It's such a comforting thought to know, He is always there to support us, even during times we are unclear, foggy and drowning in uncertainty. Each moment we allow ourselves to just be and do our work we have unleashed another piece of divinity.

If you never learn how to jump, how will you reach for the stars?

If you are truly going to come out as who you really are in this life you've got to get so clear within your own heart about who that is and stop looking to others to affirm who you already know yourself to be. This became abundantly clear to me as I started to reach for higher aspirations and truth in my own life. I began to see that I was believing what others told me over my own knowing. When you have a dream that lives inside of you, you must come to understand that under no circumstances does someone else need to validate your dream, or for that matter believe in it. On that same token even if they did understand your vision for your life it doesn't mean they wouldn't vomit all their own fears onto your dream. It's just the way human nature works.

All I'm saying is don't let someone fear-vomit all over your dreams and then you unintentionally absorb their fear. When I tell people my dream of publishing my book, manifesting a thriving life coaching, spiritual arts and reiki business all while giving talks to people on the spiritual journey, to help motivate and inspire others to live their dreams, I'm met with half the people have a sparkle in their eye, meeting my smile in return, the other half give me that bewildered look that I once thought was doubt, but now know it more intimately as a deep longing that they wish they were brave enough to listen to their inner guidance and step outside the ordinary to find their extraordinary, too.

I've learned over time to not only share my passion and vision, but to ask people what theirs is. If at first their answer is "I don't know", which is only fear of owning their truth, I'll then ask them, "what did you love doing as a child?", it's like a magic potion that digs up their truest passions. I understand just like the next person that the world we currently live in does not necessarily lend itself to self-exploration let alone following a whimsical dream that sounds much too good to be true, but the spirit inside of me also knows that the thing we can't escape is our true calling and the very thing we came here to experience. So, I keep digging into what people really want, I let them uncover for themselves in small doses. I meet their lofty, idealistic, innocent desires with nothing, but encouragement and nurturing care. That's what we should all be doing, encouraging one another to really go for it. No limits, head first, dive right into the dream, go for it.

We should be uplifting one another, believing in one another and carrying the magic that life offers with us everywhere we go. To lose hope is to lose ourselves. We were built upon hope and we must do everything we can to keep it within us and not search for it outside of ourselves. Hope is the very foundation of a life well lived. In hope, you have everything. Hope is the butterfly who was once fighting its way out of the cocoon to find itself meeting the freshly bloomed spring flower for the first time. It's the bird outside your window giving you its song. A song they sing as a gift, a melody that only they can share, telling you their story. We don't always listen to the miracles around us. Our spirits should be tended to just like the beautiful gardens we tend to grow ever magnificent within our sight. Our spirits need nourishment to rise-up to meet the desires buried deeply within our souls. We are innately worthy of our dreams coming true. Not just some of us, but all of us. Connecting to spirit is our life-line to turn our dreams into our reality. You can either choose to walk through life barely getting by or choose to walk hand in hand with your Maker along the path together. The choice is yours, it always was.

There is divinity in each one of us showing us the way if we would only listen. Sometimes listening requires us to not worry about what anyone else thinks and instead continue along our path despite any difficulties, pitfalls, or pain to keep walking towards a better way of being. God gives us exquisite, unique desires in our hearts to be fulfilled. He only gave your dreams to you because you're the only one who has the unique gifts and abilities to fulfill your destiny. You have every conceivable right, ability, and talent to do what it is you were born for. He would never give you a dream in your heart that He wasn't going to allow you to fulfill.

Yes, sometimes we might fall before getting there – a dozen times even, but eventually we will get there. It's in the rising, in the not giving up that miracles are born, stars are aligned and ordinary lives become exquisitely extraordinary. I know this to be true in my soul. I often wonder if before we came here to Earth, we set out our life's experiences and we made a promise to God that no matter what was thrown our way we would continue down our path to meet Him at the very point in which our largest obstacles became our biggest teachers and in turn became the greatest blessings to others. What keeps me going on particularly rough days is the knowing that God entrusted me with gifts that I said I would use. And I've got to use them. I just must. It's why I'm here. There is no other way for me to live.

I long to stand before my Creator at the end of my life and have Him be proud of me for believing in Him even when it was hard and believing in myself to do my work even when I didn't know how it was going to come together or what exactly it was supposed to be. To know that choosing love more often than fear made a difference. To know that in some small way, I chose my dreams more often than my nightmares, and followed my heart more often than my head.

At the end of the day, experiencing our biggest fears helps us to escape from them. As if we release them and let them go back where they came from. Surely, they were never meant to live inside of us forever. When we can say a sincere, "thank you" to our fears we know we are ready to move beyond the limitations of them. It helps us to grow and change in the way that only fear can teach us. When we have a sense of humor about our fears they no longer have any control over us.

In short, I want to face my God at the end of my time here on Earth and say, "wow, I did it God." I stood up and I was seen for all that I am and all that I know You are. I however, do not want to stand before my biggest love, my greatest supporter, my God and say, "I just couldn't do it." and have Him tell me, "Yes you could have my darling, I gave you all these unique gifts and you didn't use them to make the world a better place." I just can't bear the thought of disappointing the greatest love of my life who has given me everything I have and am. So, I will surrender to working in partnership with Him instead of fighting my gifts, I will rise-up to meet them. Will you join me in the rising?

God doesn't require us to change overnight, but to simply take baby steps, so baby steps we must take. I can do it. You can do it. We all can do it. Believe in yourself and you will be powerful beyond measure. Diminish yourself and you will be diminished. It's time to rise – there is no better time than now. We must rise and claim our highest selves and our most brilliant destiny. It's time. There is a shift happening on the planet right now. There are more lightworkers coming and more love that is needed on this planet to lift the collective energies into a place that is not only sustainable, but enjoyable. And the best thing is, it's possible.

Your heart is your compass, your soul is your guide.

You should not look outside yourself for your direction. Your heart is designed to carry you to the experiences you want to have. Your soul on the other hand is much wiser and all knowing. With these two you can never go wrong.

We are powerful beyond measure. The power of our intentions and thoughts are unshakeable. We are all given many opportunities to choose our thoughts which in turn creates the lens with which we experience our very existence. The truth is, the more we listen to our own voice the more we allow ourselves to be free from living a life that doesn't feel like our own. In every circumstance, there is an opportunity to live life in a way that inspires you to want to wake up in the morning. Even if you're not there yet, there's something inside of you that whispers this knowing into your heart. Your heart wants to be free to follow every single wind that whispers your name. Don't ever stop exploring your own happiness. Unleash your brilliance. Let it shine through for all of us to see. It is not up to you to stay in the lines. It is up to you to draw the lines. The searching is never wasted, it's in the searching that you find your way home. Like little gems of knowledge dug up from the ground to meet you where you are, if you keep digging you'll keep finding your own truth.

When you have a dream that is manifesting itself inside of you and you're not doing anything with it, it will eventually show itself in negative ways through depression, anxiety, doubt or fear. Therefore, you are in the healthiest place when you listen to your internal compass and take action toward what the dream is trying to tell you. When you listen, and act you create peace, harmony, balance, contentment and joy in your life and in your body.

It's very easy to become distracted in life. Distractions only take us further away from what we want in life. It is much easier to live a distracted life. All the distractions help us avoid looking at the things we may not want to deal with. They may help us deal with life in the short term, but they sure won't get us where we want to go. We must ask ourselves, where is our focus and is it truly where I desire it to be?

There's only one of two outcomes, it's either leading us down the path we want for our lives or it isn't. If it's not taking us where we want to go then we have some decisions we need to make. We listen to what moves us on a deep level. We may be given guidance, direction or clarity on something, but we only really listen and take action to what moves us. If there is no energy behind what we are learning then we won't do much with it except at most ponder it, give it some good thought, and eventually go back to our old ways. It must strike us like a barrel to the chest. We must feel the desire touching the exposed parts of our being to shake us fully awake.

That's how I felt when I began diving into my life coaching courses. There was something there that moved me to believe there was a different way to live life. A much more fulfilling less hopeless way to be in this world. To believe I could accomplish things that I once would have never imagined.

Take my dream to write for example, I knew my voice needed to be heard, but not just to hear myself speak or write, but for others. I knew all the lessons learned and insights gained were not just meant for me. It would be a life lived in vain if the lessons I was learning weren't shared with others. It was in the mindset and perspective I was gaining that wanted to be shared. It was my duty and honor to share and open myself up in a way that I might not ever be comfortable with otherwise.

You reach this point where it becomes much more uncomfortable to know that you have a life carved out for you and instead you're living smaller. Have you ever felt that feeling inside where you shrink back, pretending to be smaller than you know yourself to be, where all parts of you are not being fully lived and brought to the surface? It takes a bit of buoyancy to keep popping back to the surface after you have been knocked around a few times. But the natural rising process still unfolds and occurs within you even when you don't know how. Leave the rising to time, but while you have that time take care of yourself knowing you will be yourself again. Bust through any hidden, invisible barriers you feel to be real.

I don't know a better way to live life than to dream, it's part of our birthright and what God created us to do. Dreams make the world a better place. When we feel down or depressed one of the biggest reasons is usually because we stopped dreaming or we stopped believing in the power of our dreams. The thing about dreams is, there really is no perfect timing out there. The right timing is different than the perfect timing. When we wait for the perfect timing we will wait forever. It's probable we will take our dreams to the grave if we are waiting for perfect conditions. Right timing requires doing your work even when things don't seem to be going anywhere. Often times with right timing we are waiting for God to open doors only He can open. Life can bind us, deceive us into believing what we have right now isn't it, isn't enough and that there's something better. The truth is we should appreciate what we have while we have it.

I say right now is all happening in perfect timing. The people in front of you right now are a gift. An imperfect life gives us something to learn from. Maybe there are just imperfect things that are perfect for you. I'll take the lessons, keep the love and release the rest.

I think I'm a recovering perfectionist. Thinking I must be perfect until _____ can happen or _____ can happen. Or until I'll be ready or deserving of _____. Fill in the blank with anything you want......a great relationship, to contribute to this big beautiful world in the way God intended, to write my book, and on and on it goes. I'm learning everyday to not wait. I'm enough now. I always was. And so are you. The only thing being a perfectionist does is hold us back from putting ourselves out there fully. Settling takes more energy than going after what it is you truly want. The difference is with settling you're forcing yourself to stay confined. In chasing your dreams, you're taking inspired action towards what it is you want.

> *"The big question is whether you are going to be able to say a hearty yes to your adventure."*
> \- Joseph Campbell

If you've lost your way and your dreams seem to have vanished don't fret they will come back to you. If you're someone who has always felt lost with no dreams in sight rest assured they are within you. The old adage, "Ask and you shall receive" belongs right here. Ask for your dreams to come out of hiding and they will show themselves. You need to develop an intimate relationship with your dreams. You can't expect them to pursue you if you haven't taken the time to pursue them. They are alive and need to be treated as such. Give them your attention, your time and your desires and you'll be surprised at what they'll do for you in return. They'll take you to places you never thought possible. If you're not where you want to be right now, you can either choose to walk through life feeling sorry for yourself, or do something about it. The first option isn't very freeing or empowering. The second gives you all kinds of latitude to create whatever it is you want. When we get caught up in playing a victim in our own lives there isn't much that is possible, however, when we stand up for what we want and decide to make it happen life becomes exciting again.

The biggest key to unlocking the life of your dreams is action. Action is the gateway to your dreams. We can get caught up with having hopes and dreams, but those are equally fruitless if we don't do something with the inspiration to make our dreams a reality. The real deal is that we easily get caught up with distractions. Many of these distractions we create ourselves.

I get caught up in this myself instead of using my energy towards staying the course with my projects and dreams I can easily get hijacked by the dramas of life that I willingly jump head first into. By taking a step back and being downright honest with ourselves on how we are choosing to spend our time we are able to carve out opportunities to create what we are here to do. There is work to be done to leave the world in a better place than we found it. There is no better time than now since it's all there really is anyways.

This goes back to our legacy. What legacy do you want to leave behind? What mark do you want to make on the world? Once we get into the place of taking action it becomes very empowering. When we stay in the murky waters of indecision and inaction it can take a toll on our creativity and the amount of life we live. During the writing of this book there have been periods of passionate writing and lulls riddled by fear and probably downright laziness. What I've had to do to keep moving forward is remember the big picture, I am a writer. I was born to do this, whether I sell five copies or five million, this talent that God has given me is a gift, if not to anyone else, it is to myself for no other reason than it makes me feel alive and is an expression of who I am, who God ultimately created me to be. I thank Him for the gift of gab. One of the ways I'm able to do this is to talk about everything He gives me to share as His vessel. When I work in partnership with God my life is always better. I try to stay as close to Him as I can these days with my writing. If I don't stay close to Him fear will take over and I'll be done with until I can crawl my way out of that dark hole again.

Then there's this, something that came to me as I was first stepping out on my voyage of self-discovery, we must always continue even if it's one teeny tiny step. To make this very practical we may have to stop watching TV all together, or remove Facebook from our phones, or not go to that dinner with friends tonight because we have something bigger that we are working towards. Sometimes I've taken long lulls in between writing this book to give myself space to do my internal work, but I've always known in my heart I'd come back and finish what God asked me to start several years ago when I was running on that trail.

We were all created for something, to do something, something unique to us and God, something only we can do in our own way. Half the battle is finding what that thing is and the other half is doing it. Even when I've felt stuck, unsure and downright depressed I kept going. Even if it was one step one week and another the next. Taking those baby steps is what unglues our feet from the same position we've been standing in for days, weeks, months or maybe even years. There is something in the sticking that longs to be released, and when it can't all be done overnight, take those baby steps during the day. Each baby step will lead to larger steps until eventually you're where you always dreamed you would be, doing what you were created to do. But first, my darling, you must believe it before you'll see it. There's work that needs to be done there for most of us. We often think, oh well, I'll believe it when I see it, but oh no, that is not how the Universe responds to your pleas. You must first create the inner world you desire to experience the outer world you crave.

During those days when you don't feel so good about yourself or feel like giving up think about everything you've already gotten through in your life. Life isn't just about getting through it. It's about living it, feeling it, breathing it all in until your last breath. When I would get nervous to go up and speak in front of a crowd I would tell myself, "remember you were made for this." It might be scary, but I was made to do this and speaking to others makes me feel alive. We must find our inner strength during moments of doubt. To give myself some perspective and breathing room when I have to speak in front of others, is to remind myself, I've already given the most important speech of my life during my dad's eulogy. I've already braved that making everything else after a piece of cake. It was also one of the greatest honors of my life.

During those moments where you're scared out of your mind, it would be much easier and more convenient to not do that thing that stresses you out. Do it anyways. You'll be happy you did. Make a game out of it if you must. Take a step back and laugh at how worried you get when something comes up that is important to you. Then take a deep breath, put on your biggest, widest smile and rock it! Rock it! You've got what it takes, you always have! Get out there and do that thing that scares you to death and rock it.

This reminds me of getting my motorcycles license. In 2012, I was having a year of saying "yes" to every adrenaline inducing activity that came my way. When the idea of getting my motorcycles license was brought up to me I said another hearty "yes." Looking back a few years later I'm still somewhat surprised that I signed up with little to no hesitation. You must understand something here, those who really know me would probably say I'm not the best driver in general. I've never been able to master driving a stick shift after several failed attempts at being taught.

Walking into my motorcycle class the first night was amusing at best. Here I am showing up to class with a flower headband and a frilly dress on to meet the rest of the group. Most of which had a tattoo… or twelve… along with a look in their eye that said they had led a somewhat different life than me. There were a few other women in the class which was nice to see, but I have to admit I was the odd girl out. The instructor and rest of the class were great about it, had fun with it and by the time we were ready to get out on the range to start driving I was equally pumped up and nervous to ride for the first time. The bike weighed more than I expected. Simply keeping it upright was a challenge for me at first, but as the day went along I was doing better than I imagined I would. One of the instructors would call me a "biker babe" as a term of endearment to keep going when I conquered an exercise that was obviously outside my comfort zone.

I began to feel more confident within myself as I stood up on my bike and drove over 8 X 4 pieces of wood that were planted on the driving range for us to learn how to properly handle obstacles in our way. After going over and over those pieces of wood that stood in our way, it hit me that obstacles are put in our path for us to learn how to overcome them. They also help us build our confidence and our ability to take on more in the future. When the first day of training ended I went home tired and worn out but equally proud of myself for doing it. As I drifted off to sleep that night I couldn't believe where life had taken me because I had let it.

I woke up the next morning with more anxious nerves than the day before. I quickly realized it had something to do with it being motorcycle license test day. Although I had been doing a good job with our exercises I still

Faith Walk 57

had jitters that didn't always play along nicely with my driving skills, like the time I had dropped the bike the day before because I turned slightly to look over my shoulder as I was standing still waiting for my turn. As I got dressed for class and grabbed my bike helmet I began to doubt whether this was a good idea or not. Everyone else in class had already been driving bikes for years and many had taken a hiatus and let their license expire or just wanted a refresher before getting back on the road. I didn't fit any of those groups. This class was the first time I'd ever ridden a bike in my entire life. I wondered if I was going to be able to get my license today. The figure eight at the end of the test looked hard at best. Nonetheless, I got my stuff together, listened to Beyoncé on the way to class, and pretended like I was one tough chick in a rock video. Hey whatever it takes, right?

Once I hit the parking lot for the second day of class I was pleasantly surprised to see that I felt calmer. First things first, we were going through a practice test before the real deal. During the practice, the instructors would have you go back and redo a part of the test if you made a mistake that would cause you not to get your license. Both instructors were great and I could feel their encouragement. When it came time to take my test I was doing pretty good. I was doing my best to stay calm and to remember what we were supposed to do on each portion of the test. Then came the curve portion where we had to drive 15 to 20 miles then slow down to take the curve within the lines established on the driving range. I felt confident enough since I had done this same thing several times the day before and got to practice in the morning before the test. It was my turn. All eyes were on me. The two instructors and the fourteen others in the class. As I rounded the corner to take the curve I lost my balance and drove out of the lines. The instructors came over to me to let me know what they had just seen. I knew I made a mistake, but didn't realize it would cost me so many points on the test. I hadn't passed the test because I went outside the lines. Which I'm normally a proponent of in other areas in life, but on this particular piece of the test going outside the lines would mean I didn't pass with the rest of my class. I had two choices. I could either come back another time to try to retest or I could give up on getting my motorcycles license altogether. On the one hand, my ego was feeling pretty deflated. I was embarrassed I didn't pass and felt like I failed. Did I really want to show back up again with another group and potentially fail again? After all, I had signed up for the enjoyment of pushing myself outside my comfort zone not to necessarily get a bike and drive it on the open streets. Unless I got a cute little Scooter to tool around in. I wasn't sure what to do, but I did know one thing. At least I tried.

I let a week go by before I got my spunk about it back and called to reschedule my test. I decided it was important for me to follow through. The last test taught me that I let my nerves get the best of me. This time I told myself it would be different. And frankly I was too stubborn to give up when I knew in my heart I could do it. So back to the range I went. I passed that time and attributed it to staying calm under pressure and not being so hard on myself if it didn't go the way I wanted it to. It felt good to get the certificate that I passed. My instructors were so great and celebrated right along with me. The best part of all was during the celebration I received an award for the biker who was most likely to wear pink. You see they did get me after all!

Why do I share this story? For no other reason than to say, go do the things you want to do whether they are outlandish or not, whether people would be surprised you would be interested in them or not. Being open to doing something you never thought you would is a fun way to experience life and yourself in a different way. To this day I still haven't driven a motorcycle since getting my license, but any time I think back to having done it, it puts a big smile on my face. Not just thinking about it, but doing it. These experiences allow us to be able to look back during moments when we have doubt and remind ourselves we've done other challenging things. What is in front of us is no different. Plus, it was a great experience and a good learning lesson that we are all more alike than we are different. The average person may not think I belong among a pack of bikers, but I learned the opposite is true. We all belong where the wind takes us. We belong because we are people trying to get by. Those bikers had family they cared about, dreams they wanted to fulfill and fears they were overcoming. Just like me. They had a journey ahead of them and a story behind them. Just like me. I belonged among the bikers and they belonged among me. Several months later, I was at an event in small town Nebraska when a big group of bikers showed up. The first thing I did was mingle my way over to them telling them how cool their bikes were. I was welcomed as if I was one of them. Because I was. We are all people first, hobbies second.

Come out, come out, wherever you are.

We are in a day and age where we are evolving as a species. More and more people are finding the traditional way of life to be unfulfilling leaving little room for personal creativity. More and more people are wanting to leave a personal mark on humanity and make an impact in the way they are meant to. We are all born with goodness within us and part of this is wanting to contribute to others in a unique way. At the end of the day the truth is there are no guarantees in life whether we stay in one that looks safer. There is always risk in life. Risk that the job you've worked at for years will suddenly go away, the relationship you were betting on lasting the long haul suddenly drifts apart, or the clean bill of health is no longer. Why not choose to take the chances in life that are worth taking now before it's too late? Things change, life moves forward, and it's up to us to move forward with it. It really comes down to this: How do you want to live your life?

We can tend to think that the stable, straight and narrow plan for our life is the best plan, but that's not always true. Safety is not the same as being alive. Safety does not always do the thing for us as we think it does. Sometimes being safe is the worst thing for us. I talk to so many people who spill their beans to me about their dreams. This is the part where you need to listen carefully. Their truest dreams are almost never what they are doing with their lives at the moment. I've come across a very select few that say they are doing exactly what they have always dreamed of. I began to think that there must be some correlation to our dreams and not thinking we have the ability to achieve them. There must be an innate fear that our dreams are these farfetched radical ideas that our mind conjures up so we steer clear. It's as if we are so afraid of living the dream that we push it so far down that the only way it dares rise to the surface is to fester inside of us making us uneasy and eventually sick enough to the point that it spills out of us in unhealthy ways such as regret, depression or an overall lack of aliveness. The lack of following our dreams turns into manifested illness simply try to get our attention. To wake us up. But when the depression or anxiety still isn't giving us a clue that we are on the wrong path our dreams will go to more desperate measures. We'll start becoming unhealthier until one day we hit rock bottom and have no other choice, but to give it over to God and start listening.

I'm here to tell you that this is not the way it is meant to be. It's not the way God intended it to be. We associate dreams with a broken promise. The only reason it's fun to dream is so we can remove ourselves from our current reality. To follow our dreams takes a choice, a new decision to go in a new direction. One we are unfamiliar and uncertain of, one we often say "no" to before we even give it a chance. By saying "yes" we will have new skill sets to learn and embark on a new journey that we have no idea where it will lead. We can get caught up in the uncertainty of taking those first steps or we can get committed to taking them no matter what lay ahead.

The concept of failure as I hear it most often described is not the truth in my heart. We throw around this term so freely. If we take a risk and it doesn't go the way we thought, or it doesn't result in forward movement as our society describes it, monetarily or otherwise, we are quick to slap a label on it and call it failure. Every time I hear this word I cringe from the inside out. The lessons alone are movement forward. When we say we failed we just threw the whole experience away and didn't gain what we were meant to. There will be learning involved, maybe we wouldn't make the same decisions again in the future if the outcomes didn't go our way, but who wants everything our way anyways? It would make for a far less interesting life. I say kick failure to the curb. It's all living. It's all life and it's all valuable. Failure holds us captive. Learning does not. True failure would never be trying in the first place. If you put your heart and soul into something, and believed in it with all your heart. This is never failure.

If I could give anyone one piece of advice it would be to chart your own path; to not get involved with living by other people's terms, but instead fully embrace your own inner knowing. God gives us intuition, which is the greatest gift we are given. He has connected us with His divine knowing and wisdom much in the same way nature intuitively knows what to do depending on the seasons of life. God gave us an inner knowing and compass for the various seasons in our own lives. Each day we are given a new opportunity to either tap into our intuition and grow closer to our Creator or step further away by not trusting the voice within. God wants us to be His co-creator in our lives. When we trust in Him, He will lead us down paths we never imagined. Some good and some downright necessary. God doesn't live in the formality of time like we do. God simply wants us to follow His lead, knowing no boundaries to the limitless life He will give us.

Right now, in the world we exist, God is knocking on so many people's hearts, waiting for them to become more enlightened, more conscience of Him and more open to love and living in new and different ways. As a world right now we are lacking healing, forgiveness and unconditional love, which opens Pandora's box to all sorts of unhealthy emotions and ways of being. Hatred is not something we are wired to extend to others; it's created from the sense of being alone and not connected to our Creator. Many of us right now are feeling a deep sadness here on Earth because we have a remembrance of what it is like on the other side. To be with God is the ultimate feeling of love and wholeness, to be removed from the feeling of His constant presence is the worst feeling of homesickness one can imagine. It can feel like the ultimate separation from the one Who loves us more than anything, the one Who provides peace to our souls. Enlightenment teaches us that separation is an illusion. We are fully connected to God now. Feel like we are separated and lonely, asking what are we here for? Why did we choose to come here to Earth to experience this pain? We came here to learn, to grow, to understand that we can find that feeling of love and connectedness here on Earth.

Some of us were sent here with important soul missions to bring enlightenment to Earth, which has for the most part been a very dark place. If you are reading this book right now I know in my heart that it's because there is something you are meant to learn from this writing. And this might be worth it right here. Close your eyes right now, place your hand on your heart and remind yourself where you come from. You'll intuitively know, you'll sense it, you'll feel it in the depth of your existence.

The loveliest part of it is you can still connect to where you came from whenever you choose. God is with you, in you, there for you, whenever you ask. The closer to fear you are the further away from God you are, that's why there is a disconnect, not because He isn't there, but because your focus is on something else besides Him.

Life brings you seeds of inspiration, kernels of hope, moments of creativity, flashes of brilliance; take these and run with them. Don't let them float by in the breeze. Recognize them for the gifts they are. These are gifts from Heaven trying to help you from the other side. These are drops of gold trying to steer you in the right direction. The direction of your passion. Take these gems that want to burst into existence. And run wild with them. Find out where they are coming from, why they are there and what you are supposed to do with them.

I've been having these moments lately, where I have this feeling, this clarity, this truth that bubbles to the surface and in an instant, I know I must use the motivation when it comes. There is something trying to be born through you when this happens. Do the things you loved to do as a child: to write, to paint, to talk, to ride a bike, to eat ice cream. To live. Dig deeper for the truth that lives inside. The truth to your life, to all our lives. Run with it. Follow it. Create it. That thing that keeps bubbling over, don't suppress it. Chase it.

Now I'm going to speak to you directly from my soul to yours. A message I know all of us need to hear. A message from God Himself. The other night I woke up from a dream that was so real and so beautiful I had to jot it down before my mind would allow me to forget it. In the dream, I was standing off to the left of a stage getting ready to talk to a crowd of people. I felt so loved, so appreciated and had something God was telling me to share with His people. It was two words. It was simple yet powerful coming from the One Himself. The two words that God told me to share with His people were "It's Possible." In my dream, I knew people needed to hear these words. If these were the only two words uttered out of my mouth, these were the only two words that mattered.

We all need to know it's possible. That dream in your heart, that life that you would love to live, the changes you so desperately want to make in your life. It's possible. Getting out of an abusive situation, creating a better life for your family, taking that dream vacation, following your heart, living a life off the beaten path, healing from traumatic situations, finding love, being proud of yourself, owning your own business, going back to school to get a degree, or accomplishing your dreams. It's all possible. But you must believe in your own heart it's possible to take the first steps. You will have to trust there is something greater than you at play. You will have to find the strength within yourself to make the change. But it's possible.

I was talking to a friend the other day about my subconscious belief that I need to struggle. While I wish it were easy for me to flip the switch and let go of that belief and change it overnight to be on my merry way, I must first and foremost give it over to God to allow Him to take my struggles and transform them into raindrops that fall at my feet. My reality has been that I've had to look at my life, my patterns and my desires for an easier way to let go, bit by bit of those old belief patterns that have held me back. If we are looking for a magic bullet I'm afraid it just doesn't exist, my dears. But what does exist is our ability to be more forgiving of our pain, and consciously invite and allow more moments of peace, clarity and love into our everyday lives. When we notice we are once again relying on our old patterns to get us through we have to realize we have the power and the choice to drop the old and pick up the new once again. It's possible.

I have struggled, deeply. Probably like many of you. I have struggled through the loss of a parent much too soon. The end of a marriage. The pain of losing everything I loved to follow a path that didn't work out for me. I have felt depression and despair. Yes, there have been struggles. And I'd take each one all over again. Because I have evolved out of those struggles. I have seen the light again. I have felt the fire and still managed to get up every day knowing it would all lead to something better. I have been where you have been and I'm telling you to keep going. Somedays I wish I could say I'm the girl that doesn't struggle, but then I realize I wouldn't change a thing because instead of being the girl that doesn't struggle I'm the girl who overcomes her struggles. That resonates with my soul so much more. It's life. It's what I came here to do, to live, to learn, to love, and to feel pain.

During those times when change has so abruptly taken over my life I needed time to mourn my losses to make room for the new to enter. Simply put, dreams show us what we are meant to do here, if we didn't dream it, it wouldn't be possible for us. The fact that a true, authentic dream comes to us is a nudge that this is part of why we are here. If you can dream it, you can achieve it. This kind of dream is persistent in its quest to awaken the part of you that's been asleep. Whether you choose to awaken from your slumber is up to you.

Chapter Five

The Purpose in Your Calling

> *"I believe there's a calling for all of us. I know that every human being has value and purpose. The real work of our lives is to become aware. And awakened. To answer the call."*
> -Oprah

I'll never forget the day I gave my life over to God. It was the same day He unveiled my calling.

Our calling is that thing that beats us over the head relentlessly, that we can try to run from, but it will always end up a step ahead of us waiting for us to pass through it. Changing our lives as we do. Ultimately our calling is simply trying to call us home to ourselves. I tend to talk about purpose a lot. I feel such conviction about what my purpose is and once I found it my life completely changed. I now had a roadmap of what I wanted to accomplish in my life. Suffice it to say I've had a lot of conversations around purpose. I've had others ask me, "What do you think my purpose is?" My response is always something like this, "Have you asked God what it is yet?" I usually get a "no" as the response.

We each have the ability to ask God what it is and He wants to help answer that question for us. If I hadn't asked Him and then heard so resolutely what the answer was I may not have walked this path. We must get in the habit of not having to rely on ourselves for all our answers, they are within us, God is there to help guide us and provide us with information when the time is right. My darlings, I ask you to quiet your mind, open your heart and ask away. When you do this with an honest quest you will be amazed at the support, guidance and wisdom you receive. It will change your path, chart your course and it will be the one thing you can't run from no matter how hard you try. Your call wants to be expressed through you and it will be so powerful you will not be able to escape it. Nor will you want to, it will be the thing that's buried so deep within your heart you will naturally long for it. If you've got something important to share you will be asked to share it and rightfully so. We are meant to contribute our gifts to others so that they may evolve through our experiences that somehow mirror their own. It is our duty to take care of one another. It is a privilege to share what we are learning so that others may learn as well. Our knowledge is most valuable when we learn it for the whole instead of keeping it to ourselves.

When I think about all the amazing inventors, truth seekers, light bearers, way makers and brave hearts that gave their gifts to this world I can't help but think that the beautiful tapestry of life we get to live in is partly because of them. Life just wouldn't look or feel the same if they hadn't stepped up to give us their courage instead of their fear. When I think about my life and all the pleasures I delight in, books I adore, movies I find my own story in, or poetry that carries my soul's language, I am eternally grateful for the ones who stood up and stood out by listening to their calling especially in the midst of doubt. It comes down to how we want to be remembered and more importantly how we want to remember our own lives. Do you want to be remembered as the person who was great at being afraid or the person who despite their fears did great things? We can all get caught up in avoiding the very things we came here to do. When we get attached to an outcome is when things take a turn for the worse. If you can conquer the need to know how things are going to turn out and instead work towards doing good things every single day you will shift from making it about yourself to making it about doing the good deed. Introspection and self-knowledge is the key to working around any pitfalls you may have.

Commit to your purpose and watch your life come alive.

Avoidance is not the answer to creating a better, brighter world. Commitment is. Commitment knows no boundaries. Commitment is what will carry you through the dark night of the soul and transcend you to the other side where your calling lives. When we are committed we show up as a warrior for a cause. When we are noncommittal we can be blown over by the faintest of ocean breezes. To commit is to know you will make it through to the other side, that you will see your story through until the end. No matter what is shown on the surface you have a certainty inside knowing that the winds of change will not change your commitment to your path.

The downfall with not learning to commit is that you'll move in a different direction as often as the seasons change and by nature nothing has the chance to evolve or develop roots in that kind of time frame. What you'll be left with is your life constantly being uprooted without the chance of coming to fruition. We must commit to our calling. You can either commit to your calling or commit to the chaos and drama in your life, but you can't have both. You must commit every single piece of who you are to it. You cannot commit a fraction of yourself to it. You cannot think you can commit only pieces of yourself to it and think anything fruitful will come out of it. You must commit all parts of yourself to it. The parts that are safe, the parts that like to stay away from risk, the parts that question if you're doing the right thing. This is the way it works when you have a true calling to do something bigger than yourself. You can't dabble in it for ten minutes here or fifteen minutes there and call it a calling. That's called a hobby or a pastime. A calling takes dedication. It lives in you every second of every day taking up residence in every fiber of your being. It will haunt you until your insides become raw by the thought that you may never fulfill it.

A calling grips you in the middle of the night and whispers into your ear as a reminder that you haven't answered it yet and still it's waiting. The call will wait to be answered until the very moment that you die if you let it. Or you can choose to get on with it, embrace it, figure out a plan and play nice with it. Give your call the amount of time necessary to develop it into something deep, meaningful and ultimately more beautiful than the alternative. When we look at our lives and all we see is surface with nothing much below it's an indication that we haven't found any depth yet. Depth is what sustains us, surface is what keeps us from growing any deeper than where we've been planted.

Have you ever felt that feeling that you're barely getting by? I have. During these times I ask myself, "where is it I want to go" and "why am I not going towards it?" If you feel like you're on that all too familiar hamster wheel it's probably because you are. This is a good indicator that there is something fundamentally not on par with your true nature and you're not yet ready to look it in the face and make much needed changes. Why? Because change is hard for the vast majority of us. It's all in how we view change. With change comes the threat of it shaking our world up. Because of this we may choose to avoid change all together. Change is uncertain and most of us don't like to feel uncertain. The old saying goes, "I'd rather live with the devil I know instead of the devil I don't know." I'd rather look at it like I'm following spirit every day. If spirit is leading me towards change I must be open to trying. There is one thing I know for certain. We all want meaning. We want to experience life and live it for ourselves not through someone else's lens. We need to find our meaning and then never let it die. We may have different purposes at different points in our lives, but the quest to find it must always stay alive for without it there is no purpose.

There came a day when I realized part of my meaning was helping others get through loss. The thing about our purpose is that we don't choose it, it chooses us. Even in the choosing it doesn't always come along out of a nice story it comes out of the parts of our story that are broken. Our purpose is born out of our ashes.

The biggest wounds create the most beautiful reasons for existing. We never truly know what God is going to call us to do yet our passions arise from the things that are dearest to our hearts. I've always loved writing, but it wasn't until I felt I had something valuable to share that I knew I could take my love of writing and help heal other people's wounds. We are not meant to go through struggles only to keep the healing and learning to ourselves, we are meant to share the healing with others who aren't as far along the path as we are. If God gives you understanding and wisdom you're surely meant to give it as a gift to others. For every issue there is in this world God gave us people who know how to fix it. The question then becomes whether we are going to step up and do something with what we've been given. Get your why figured out and then move towards it. Why is it important for you to do what you were brought here to do?

I've often asked myself what is the story of my life going to be? Well, I'm living it. Right here, right now just like you. How can we live life with more purpose and passion? I've pondered this question repeatedly asking myself, "What is my purpose?" In asking myself this question I have realized that I, as well as everyone else, have many purposes. One of mine is to write and share my story. A calling never leaves you. It will stay with you and knock at your door until you decide to let the call in. Once you invite it in it will stay with you day after day and consume your thoughts until you take action. That's the gift of the call it will never leave your side. It's game on from there, you've given it permission to absorb itself into your very being.

You cannot walk in darkness forever. You can't hide from your brilliance long term. You must turn to the light eventually. The light is always there to illuminate your path. We can get caught up in not wanting to be fully seen. Because it is in being fully seen that we have the ability to become who we really are. I've spent enough time hiding, have you? Hiding from who you really are and how incredibly gifted and loved you are. The work you are meant to do here is not going anywhere. You are called to be one with yourself, the call is part of you. We all have purpose within us. Purpose is a word that caught fire. There's a reason for that, we are all searching for it, which shows us how much we've grown on this planet. Some of us were meant to lead the way. To go through certain difficult life events to pave the way for those who will come after. Stand up to your own greatness and show the next generation how it's done. Don't you want to be that parent or family member that shows the kids who are growing up today that they don't have to follow the well beaten path and do the things in life you didn't enjoy yourself? Show them that living a life you truly love is possible. Teach them that they live with purpose inside of them and it doesn't come in the form of how big their paycheck is or the college they get into. It comes in the size of their heart, the depth of their faith and the zest for life they choose to let in.

We all look for purpose in our lives. We want to find that one magic bullet that will make everything better. Unfortunately, the magic bullet doesn't exist. We must do the work to get where we want to go. As a people, when are we going to stop talking about what we want and instead go out there and live it? I promise you that you do not want to wake up one day knowing you could have fulfilled your inner voice and you chose not to. Don't we all long to leave our mark on the world? Working an eight to five may or may not be that for you. Really look at what it is you're contributing and ask yourself if it's going to make a difference to someone in five, ten, fifteen years down the road. If the answer is yes, good work. If the answer is no, you may want to reassess what you're doing with your life.

One of the most difficult parts of following your path is that you may not have a lot of other people on it. If you want to truly step out on your own and do something extraordinary and unique you'll have to get comfortable standing on your own two feet. Sometimes that means not giving into the comforts of staying where you are. To evolve we must never get idle with where we are. If God has something specifically for you to do, He will move you where he needs you to go to accomplish it. At some point in your life you must decide to follow the voice within if you're ever going to become who you might have been. It's really a matter of what the soul desires. We may not understand on a mental level why we are being called forth to begin walking down a new path, but our souls have always known the longing of our hearts desire. Our soul has always known what it wanted to accomplish and experience during this lifetime; more importantly what we were brought here in the first place to do with our time. If you never decide to listen to the longing of your own soul it will be a shame because your soul would not be able to be fully expressed through your being. Our soul remembers everything. It holds all of the contents of our lifetimes. With the amount of depth and knowledge we have as humans, it's impossible not to recognize that we don't get this amount of wisdom by being here on Earth once.

As we evolve what we are meant to contribute to the world will also evolve. It's very easy to get stuck in a rut and find ourselves doing the same thing for so long that we become incorrectly attached by what we think is our identity. We identify ourselves with such fleeting things such as our jobs, our relationships we're in or even our bank account or possessions, when none of these things have anything to do with who we really are. What we all want is to experience our own essence during this lifetime in everything we do, think or spend time and resources on as an extension of our being. When we act in accordance with our true nature we are at peace. However, when we spend any of these energies doing something that is not in alignment with who we really are, it creates unease and internal conflict. The only way we are able to get back to a peaceful state is to follow our hearts knowing about who we really are and how we would like to experience ourselves. This is the key to success and happiness. When we show up in our lives as our highest versions of ourselves we experience life at a higher vibration where true joy, compassion and kindness live. The more peaceful you are with yourself the more you experience this state of being.

When you decide to go down your path you will inevitably face roadblocks. Our spirituality and beliefs are a personal matter that only we have the power to change. It's not wrong to share your beliefs or engage in dialogue to open your mind and heart to what it is you are searching for, but it is wrong to be told what to believe or judge others for their beliefs. My journey has taught me that spirituality is like anything else. Once we go down the road towards learning and evolving we must peel back layer upon layer of conditioning and old belief patterns to find what we truly resonate with. I've never been one to tell someone what they should or should not believe in. I believe in quite the contrary, that you should have the freedom to find what works for you. This is exactly what I have done in my life. Taking bits and pieces of many things that resonate with me and carrying them with me as my truth. They all lead back to the one true God. I liken it to languages. There are many languages and ways of communication. Whichever one works for you to get as close a connection to God as you can is the right one for you.

When things don't touch me as truth I keep searching. When I find something that sparks my interest I follow it. Each time I have followed my truth it has led me to continual learning about new things I never would have experienced if I hadn't kept an open heart and mind. I have found many things I deeply resonate with as truth down to my soul. This is one of the true gifts in life. We have the ability to continually expand our hearts and our minds, even in small doses.

For some of us we may find God in a religion, for others we may find Him in our backyards or at our kitchen tables. For me, I used to think, I found Him most in nature because I thought I could hear Him better in the silence until I realized He's found inside of me every moment of every day. I take Him everywhere I go and in everything I do. We've got it all wrong. We try to go "somewhere" to find Him when in reality He's everywhere and everything. He's in the sunshine in the morning on your drive to work, He's in the disagreement you just had with a friend, He's in the homeless man's eyes meeting yours on the side of the road, He's in every thought you have and every breath you take. He doesn't care where you go to find Him, He's only concerned that you do find Him, that you remember where you came from, and that you return to His unending love for you. Sometimes He's a little louder to get our attention, other times He's quiet just to see if we will grow closer to Him in our trust for the plans He has for us even when He is silent. It's amazing the miracles that He will bring into your life if you let Him and the person He will shape you into if you trust Him.

I never in a million years would have imagined I would become a writer and to write about my spiritual journey towards faith through trials and heartbreak. This wouldn't have been what I envisioned my life plan to be. It's so much bigger than I would have dreamed for myself. It was only after facing the greatest loss of my life to date that I uncovered or maybe rediscovered my calling. I'm a lover of God and all His people. It's really that simple. I don't identify myself as believing in one specific religion or dogma. I consider myself to be a very spiritual being who believes and is open to many paths as long as they all lead back to our beautiful Creator. It's like I get to have a relationship with Him in many different forms and variations. I'm a student. I'm constantly learning. I know what it's like to follow that faint whisper up ahead in the distance beckoning me to continue to explore the parts of myself that I haven't met yet.

Take my time at the Ashram for example. I had several experiences there, some better than others. As I continued to search I began to open up parts of myself, as if there was a familiar knowing of the land from lifetimes before, rituals I so easily picked up. There was no way I hadn't done this before. One of the biggest things my time at the Ashram taught me was that you can take anything you want and blend it together and not have to figure out how it works in tandem with other beliefs and just simply know that it does. I've become a blender of things that resonate with me. Because in the end there really are no rules to anything in life and certainly not to our beliefs.

As humans, we like to make up rules because it helps us to feel more comfortable with the internal struggle. We want to know things for certain that are truly uncertain. I'd rather live by my gut instinct if something is true for me. If a spiritual practice makes me feel more connected and closer to God then I can't possibly fathom why it would be a bad thing. Especially when it all leads back to the same thing.....God. There's multiple ways to worship and meet God. Waking up on top of a mountain at 4:30 in the morning to ring in my 33rd birthday with God waiting for me to surrender my life over to Him fully and completely in silence and prayer was one of the happiest times my heart has ever felt. My heart felt so big and so full it could burst out of my chest at any moment. And then there was the time I found my way to a quaint little book store in Boulder where I plopped myself down right in front of the spiritual section where I sat all night sifting through every spiritual book imaginable with a thirst I couldn't quench to learn about my Creator through other people's eyes. The most important thing I've learned about all these experiences is that God asks us to find Him ourselves, not only through a book, or a story, but by creating an authentic relationship with Him. He wants us to come to Him ourselves with our hearts wide open to experience who He is for ourselves. Once you surrender your life over to Him He will show up in a way you never would have imagined. The love you will feel is a love like no other. His love only scratches the surface of the love we feel here on Earth.

It's the kind of overwhelming love that only He can provide. We all have the opportunity to receive it.

Enlightenment is not a place we evolve to, it's a brief stroke of magic that we stumble upon occasionally if we're lucky. We are all teachers. We are brought here to learn lessons and help others learn theirs. We each signed up for roles in each other's lives, some big, some small. However, each role has its own significance. I look for meaning in everything from the mundane happenings to the bigger moments because nothing is ever meaningless. Life itself is full of meaning. It's up to us to find what's meaningful for us. Don't be afraid of doing your own soul searching to find what is meaningful for you.

When I was first starting to believe fully in God and that my loved ones were still with me on the other side, my mind would try to rationalize my ability to connect with them on the other side, while my heart was telling me it was true. The way I was conditioned to believe was keeping me stuck from really digging into my spiritual gifts. Your beliefs may be completely different than the norm or than how your family raised you, but don't let that stop you from pursuing your truth. Let the truth spill out of you so clearly that you will never be the same as you were before stumbling upon it.

As I continued to follow my spiritual path I found people who had traveled a similar road before me and they became my mentors. I truly became blessed by the people God put on my path. They were people who were open, encouraging and some were twenty steps ahead of me waiting for me to catch up. Those were the relationships that really helped me become my true self.

You can't undo your purpose by any mistakes you've made or decisions you wish you hadn't made. You can try to push it away, but even still it will come find you, to knock at the door of your heart until you open it even a crack, to let it in. Your purpose is so patient that it will wait patiently for you to be ready to run with it. Our purposes may change over time, but the true essence of what our soul longs to do will always be there at our doorstep waiting patiently to be picked back up again. You can even ditch your purpose, defriend it and it will still remain true to you. It will ask for forgiveness and return to your side and be the spotlight of your life once again. There is no higher calling than to listen to the whispers of your own heart. Within your heart lies all the wisest, truest answers to your most real, authentic, juicy, adventurous life. The one you came here to live. Purpose gets through to us each in a different way. For me it was the deep knowing, the yearning, the relentless restlessness that ensued any time I wasn't listening and taking action in the direction of my purpose. It has been my brightest hopes and my biggest fears. It's the heart wrenching realization that if I don't continue to follow that nagging voice my soul will wretch in agony. In the trying we show the Universe we are accepting our destiny and the One who created all things. In the accepting of the purpose we are able to release the fear around having the life we were created to live.

The amount of fear that surrounds doing the things that are the most meaningful to us is astounding in our culture. We chase after things that are unfulfilling and inauthentic to who we really are instead of the life we long for and then we wonder why so many of us end up depressed, drug down and disenchanted with life. Our society has a lot of soul searching to do on a collective level. The ones who are brave enough to chase their dreams are cautioned to do anything other than the norm because the norm supposedly leads to safety and assurances yet nothing is safe or secure. None of us are in control, yet we cling to things that no longer serve us because we are more afraid to not know what the future holds than to risk leaving what no longer calls to our souls so that we can feel some semblance of assurance. There's no heart in that. There's no love in that. There's no life in that. We stay in relationships, jobs and commitments past their expiration date just to feel safe. Then one day something happens in our lives which will inevitably happen to everyone at some point in time that teaches us everything is temporary. If you can take the lesson for what it is, the experience will shake you awake to be braver with your life and let go of things you should a little sooner with a little more ease.

Chapter Six

Sunshine After the Rain

Shine

The sun will shine again loves
The darkness can't last forever
The moon gets tired too
The ebb and flow of life
They show us our strength, our power, our resiliency
The darkness can't last forever
The light burns brighter than the night

As I write this book that's been on my heart for years I'm experiencing discomfort. Sharing myself, revealing my innermost thoughts and beliefs on life is much more uncomfortable than I had imagined. I'm finding that I'm fine during the day when I'm writing, but then when I awake in the morning I feel vulnerable and bare. I'm not sure that I really like this feeling. I had imagined it going so much differently. I imagined I would be happy to finally be at the place where I was writing my book. I would feel free, wouldn't I? Now I'm not sure that's necessarily the case. Since our thoughts are usually different than our reality I'm certain after reading my own library of self-help and spiritual awakening books that this is just the way it is for those of us who really put ourselves out there. It's like a trapeze that flings us from bravery to fear. If you simply allow yourself to swing back and forth between the two you'll come along nicely towards your truth.

Here I am at a retreat center in the woods out in the middle of nowhere in a small Iowa town surrounded by nothing more than my own thoughts. Thoughts I've wanted to share for so long. Thoughts I am sharing now. And it's just not quite as glamorous as I expected, but then again most of the things that really matter never are. Take the time I ran the New York City Marathon in memory of my dad. It's easy to say it was in memory of my dad, which is partly true. The other part of that equation is that it was for myself. I've just never been quite as comfortable doing something for myself, which is something I'm working on. Doing it for my dad helped give me the motivation deep down inside to keep going. It's always given me more motivation to do something for someone else; maybe then I feel like I will accomplish it and see it through. There was nothing glamorous about training or finishing those 26.2 miles. Glamorous just isn't the right word. But meaningful is, fulfilling is, proud is, difficult is. Those are all words that make up part of my experience.

When I started running the year before taking on the marathon I never imagined it was preparing me for one of my biggest dreams to come true. Back when I was far from being a runner I had seen photographs of the New York City Marathon on a news website telling the stories of those who finished, why they wanted to run, what inspired them and what got them through. I was so enamored by their stories and in awe of how they had the gumption to do it. At that very moment, I tucked it in my "I would love to, but that's not for me" file and went about life. Well, that file got opened in the summer of 2013. A year after running had found its way into my life acting as my saving grace. It was July and I was ready for another adventure. When you are putting out an adventurous vibe adventure will seek you out until it finds the rightful owner. As if by divine grace, as I was sitting in my car waiting for an appointment I decided to check my e-mail. I'm not the best at keeping up with junk e-mail that seems to pile up, but on this particular day I was drawn to open an e-mail with the subject line "Cellmates on the Run." As I read through the e-mail I got that familiar feeling that would come over me when I knew I was supposed to do something.

Cellmates on the Run is an organization that works to cure diabetes. Diabetes ran on my dad's side of the family and was very near and dear to my heart since my dad, several uncles and my grandfather all had this life altering metabolic disease. In the e-mail, they were looking for runners to sign up to raise funds for research and in return you would get an entry into the Chicago Marathon. I figured Chicago would be a great first stab at my first marathon, but then when I got home that evening to register online I noticed to my utter delight and amazement that they also had entries into the New York City marathon. Talk about a surreal moment. My heart practically leapt out of my chest as tears began to run down my face when I noticed that the run would take place on November 3, 2013 a mere two days after my dad would have celebrated his sixtieth birthday. I just couldn't possibly turn this once in a lifetime opportunity down. I would get to raise money for a wonderful organization and honor my dad's life at the same time. I was all in. Never mind I had never ran more than a half marathon in my life, I was bound and determined to cross that finish line. In three short months, I would need to raise several thousand dollars, train several times a week, make the trek to New York City and run 26.2 miles. As soon as I signed up my entire focus was on making this happen.

When I told people what I was doing in such a limited timeframe some were worried for me and others pushed me right along with their enthusiasm. The thing I learned a long time ago was that if I didn't say "yes" now, when would I? Part of the key to living a full life is understanding that your fear will tell you to do it tomorrow or next month or next year because "the circumstances will be better then." The truth is you have no reason not to say "yes" now. We all can come up with a gagillion excuses. But that's different than a reason. There is no good reason to say "no" to the things in life that are the most important to you. You can make it work. When we make excuses, they weaken us. It becomes easier and easier to say "no" more and more often. We can feel the lie in the excuse and there's a small piece of us on the inside that knows we're making an excuse. Excuses feel limiting, whereas "yes" feels expanding.

Back to the marathon: I was in a place where "yes" was beaming from my being. Once I made the commitment and signed up for the run and started training and fundraising, people were excited for me. The vast majority had arrived at a place where they just knew I was going to do what I wanted so they encouraged me by asking how my training was going, donating money and sharing my story with others. It felt so good to be honoring my dad by raising money for diabetes and posting our story on the website for Cellmates on the Run.

Around this time God was teaching me a lot of lessons about myself. Things that I needed to work on. One of the big ones was asking for help and then accepting it. Allowing others to help me has never been my strong suit. Growing up I was independent and took care of myself. I had always been much more comfortable helping others versus being helped by others. This was one of the first times in my life I can remember not being able to do it alone. There was no way I was going to be able to raise the money to run without asking other people for help. Each time I sent an email or made a phone call for donations it took every ounce of me to follow through until the moment I realized this wasn't about me at all. It was about a great cause. Each person that donated was helping diabetes research and I was just the vessel God was using to make it happen. I kept expecting people to say "no" to me, but I found that most were overjoyed to help a dream of mine come true. They were inspired by my story and they wanted to help me achieve it. I also found another surprise, by sharing what I was doing, I was encouraging others to go do something they had always wanted to do.

I'll never forget one evening during my training regimen, as I was grabbing things from my car on the way in to facilitating GriefShare at my church, a gentleman walked out and asked if he could help me carry in the 24-pack of water bottles I was carrying. I was clearly struggling with carrying this along with everything else I had in my hands. My first instinct was to say, "no thanks, I've got it." But something struck me in that moment and still does today. If I couldn't say "yes" to someone helping me carry in a package of water how was I ever going to be able to say "yes" to the bigger things in life. The things I dreamed of having. In that moment of clarity, I was able to respond differently than I normally would have and said "yes, that would be so helpful, thank you!" Don't think the smaller things in life, something as simple as being helped in with water, don't add up to the bigger things. They do. God was teaching me that if I couldn't accept help, my life would be a lot more difficult, and that I was the one making it that way. I began to look at these encounters as little games. Would I pass the test of accepting help? Or would I stay bound up by my own need to keep people out instead of letting them in? Growing up as someone who never wanted to ask for much, I realized that in not allowing others to help me, I was stealing their joy and blessing in being a good person to another. I would have many more encounters like these during marathon training. Boy, does God know how to put you in circumstances where getting help is the only way to make it through.

My twelve-week marathon training began soon after I made the decision to sign up. I had a half marathon already on the calendar I had to get through in September in Omaha and then the real deal marathon training would begin. I got through the half marathon in September without much issue, but by my last long training run in October I wasn't sure I was going to be able keep up with the rigor of the training runs. The pace of the training schedule was proving to be hard on my body. My right foot, knee and hip were having trouble keeping up and it became painful to run long distances. After I would run my long run on a Sunday I could barely walk into work the next day without limping. A few weeks prior to the marathon, during my final long run of twenty-two miles, it put me over the edge. As I was running and training for the marathon I would pray to be carried to the finish line. I had this knowing that there was no way I would accomplish this on my own, but that the Lord would be right beside me, carrying me when needed. After the twenty-two mile run a few short weeks before the marathon, I made the decision to back off my training schedule in hopes I would heal some before staring down the barrel of those twenty-six point two miles on race day.

After some advice from a friend I began to see a chiropractor several times before race day. He was a nice guy and was clearly doing everything he could to get me well enough to tackle this run that he could clearly see meant the world to me. I already wasn't feeling completely sure about it and then he added fuel to the fire by cautioning me to take it easy. He told me in all honesty he didn't think I would be able to make it with my injuries and that I'd be lucky to finish the half marathon let alone the full. He just didn't think I'd be able to cross the finish line and wanted to prepare me in advance for that possibility. But luckily when someone tells me I can't do something it has always propelled me further. I think it's the stubborn girl that lives inside of me. Taking "no" for an answer has luckily never been my strong suit. I will find a way to make it happen. I said to myself, even if it was in my own head, "just watch me." I was certainly not going to take "no" for an answer on this one. This marathon had my name written all over it and my dad's, too. There was no way I wasn't going to experience it for myself. I learned that many people saw me for my sweetness, but there was an entirely different side to me as well. My sassy and stubborn sides came to my rescue that day. As they often do when something is very important to me. These traits have never failed me, it's like they show up right when I need them.

When the time came for me to set off for New York City I couldn't believe I was actually going to do this. My two dear friends, Janette and LaRonda, were accompanying me. As we arrived in the largest city in America it was time to go pick up my race packet. I was fascinated by how long it took us just to make it to the auditorium where the race expo was being held to get my bib for race day. I'll never forget standing in front of the race day countdown display to get my picture taken for prosperity's sake with a t-shirt I had made with a photo of my dad and me on it that read, "Always in my Heart." It would have been my dad's sixtieth birthday that day. I couldn't help, but smile up at Heaven knowing he was with me on this adventure. I was lucky for my dad to be a twin. I went over to see my Uncle Dan the evening before I left for New York City to wish him an early birthday and let him know I'd be running a mile for him, too. I loved my uncle like a second dad and he had helped me get through the pain of losing my dad. My dad and uncle were identical twins and like two peas in a pod. As part of my fundraising for diabetes research I had offered donors the opportunity to donate a mile to someone they loved who lived with diabetes or someone they lost. A friend put a T-shirt together for me to wear on race day with all the miles being donated except for mile 26,

I was saving that one for my dad. I ran for my uncles and my Grandpa Montgomery who had struggled with diabetes as well.

The next day, the day before the run, my girlfriends and I decided to take a tour bus to see the sights of New York City to save my legs for race day. I'll never forget the moment I looked up from the tour bus, feeling like I was being nudged just in time to see a sign that read, "Dave's Auto", right in front of me. With my dad's name being Dave I knew it was a wink from him that he was with me that day and knew exactly what I was about to embark upon. It was even more coincidental that at one point in my dad's life he owned his own auto body shop called, "Dave's Auto Repair." Funny how the Universe works, right? You just can't make this stuff up. The Universe is always giving us evidence and proof that the spirit world is very alive and real. It's up to us whether or not we are willing to listen and take in the information.

After having a fun day in the city, it was time to prepare for race day. I had to carb load and get to bed early. I knew my nerves were going to make it hard for me to sleep that night, but I also knew I'd better try. I woke up bright and early on November 3, 2013 excited that race day was finally here. I took my time making sure I had everything I'd need for the day, being sure not to take too much with me that I would have to carry those 26.2 miles. As I walked out the hotel room door I looked back on my sleeping friends feeling incredibly grateful they were with me. As I sat down in the lobby waiting to be picked up by a shuttle that Cellmates on the Run arranged for all its runners, I couldn't help but feel fortunate that I would soon be living out this dream. I appreciated how convenient Cellmates on the Run made it for their runners to get around a city that I would otherwise be lost in. The shuttle service arrived promptly at 5:30 a.m. to pick me up and take me to the holding place at the Verrazano-Narrows Bridge in Staten Island where all the runners wait for their turn to begin their long journey to the finish line. Before my wave started running, I waited at the bridge with the other 50,000 plus runners, making it the largest marathon in history, I couldn't help but think back to the day I was laying in my bed only wishing I could run in the marathon myself. And now here I was about to step over the starting line to embark upon the longest run of my life. I promised myself it wouldn't matter how the run went, it was enough that I was doing it. I would travel far that day both in steps, spirit, and internal growth. I would prove to myself that anything really is possible through commitment, faith and perseverance. Little did I know that thought would serve me well as I continued down the longest journey I'd ever taken by foot.

It was incredible to talk to other runners while we were each waiting for our wave to begin. As I was exchanging stories with another runner about what brought us both there that day, I couldn't help but be impressed that she had run multiple marathons to get to race day. Some raised money for charity to get an entry while others qualified. When she asked me if I'd ran other marathons before I said, "nope this is my first." She was surprised by the answer telling me that this was one of the more difficult races because of all the bridges, inclines and hills throughout the course. She further lamented that she had been training for five years to get to this point to take on this course. All I could do was laugh. If anyone was going to sign up for a race that she just described, on a whim no less, with three months of training under her belt it would surely be me, always leading with my heart. I figured this wasn't anything I should spend my time worrying about since I already had enough of those pre-race jitters.

Finally, my wave was called. I had been waiting in the cold November weather since 7:30 a.m. and it was now a little after 11:00 a.m. I was used to running early in the morning for the other races and mini triathlons I had done throughout the year to get me to this point. I wasn't sure how this would affect my day with not much left in my stomach as I stared down those 26.2 miles. Needless to say, when my wave lined up and I heard the gunshot signaling our start I could feel the collective anxiousness to begin. As I took my first steps across the Verrazano- Narrows Bridge I was overcome with emotion welling up inside of me. Seeing so many runners around me who were just as determined to check this dream off their list was incredible. I couldn't help but wonder what brought each one of them there that day. To choose this as a goal. But I knew I'd better concentrate on the task ahead of me and ponder that question later. When I run I have to get myself into a groove. I can't listen to music or fill my head with too many distractions. On my best days, running becomes a mediation and I'm able to get through several miles at a time without realizing how far I've gone. This was my hope for the marathon that would take us through all five boroughs of New York City. It began in Staten Island, then took us through Brooklyn, Queens, the Bronx and finished in Manhattan's iconic Central Park.

Running through those five boroughs felt like a city-wide block party that was designed to help keep the runners going. The run started off on a good note. I was in my groove and my foot, knee and hip were doing much better than I anticipated given I had only been resting them for the past few weeks. As I approached the drink stations, I remembered a piece of advice I heard from another runner before the race started. The runner had suggested that since my wave started after 11:00 a.m. without eating much except for a banana and half a bagel with some peanut butter that it would be a good idea for me to take in more Gu Energy Gel than I had during my training runs to make sure I had enough energy to finish the race. I figured it made sense and decided to take the gel every 30 minutes as suggested instead of every 45 minutes to an hour that I'd been training with. I figured this was a small decision in the grand scheme of 26.2 miles and kept on going.

I couldn't contain my enthusiasm when around mile eight while in Brooklyn, after running a portion with no spectators, rounding a corner to see thousands and thousands of people lined up on each side of the street cheering us on. The crowd had signs, noise makers, some were dressed up, but all were rooting us on towards our victory. It felt like I was in the middle of the Macy's Day parade. I had only seen crowds like this on TV never in person. I had never witnessed so many people in my life. I'm someone who always chooses to run on the outside of the crowd of runners so I feel like I have a little more space to pace myself. I couldn't help but give people in the crowd high fives as I ran along that stretch of street. It felt amazing to have so many people cheering us on. All I wanted to do was give them a little love back. By mile fifteen I could tell the last goo I had taken a mile before hadn't set well with me. As I stopped for more water and goo around mile eighteen my stomach started to ache. I could tell something was off. Here I was a little over half way through the marathon without much of a problem and the last thing I needed was for my stomach to get upset. I began to remember what I had learned when I first started running with goo the year before. You always want to take the same amount of goo during the race that you use to train with or it could upset your system. I hadn't listened to my own intuition about that and instead had been taking in way more than normal on the advice of my fellow runner. And now I was paying for it. By mile eighteen there was no longer any doubt that I was going to get full on sick on the side of the road. As I made my way over to the side of the road to get sick I couldn't help but feel proud when two runners ran past me and said, "Congratulations, you're a runner!", as I upchucked all that goo that had been swimming around unhappily in my stomach for the last four miles.

To my amazement I was able to get through the next two miles before I would need to stop to get sick again. Only this time God sent me support while I was hunched over feeling like I could literally pass out after running for twenty miles with six of those miles feeling nauseated the entire time. As if out of nowhere a gentleman appeared by my side coming over to see if I was okay. He didn't once hesitate or worry that stopping to help a sick woman on the course would put his own finish time behind schedule. Instead he showed his genuine concern by telling me I didn't look well and that he should probably take me over to one of the first aid tents. As I stood up, I thanked him for being so kind to stop to check on me. I then explained to him that there was no way I was not going to cross the finish line, that I had come too far not to and that I was doing it for my dad. I almost cried when his response was, "We'll cross the finish line together then." My first instinct was to tell him he didn't have to do that, I wouldn't want him to mess up his own finish time, while waiting on me. By the way I was feeling I wasn't sure if I could run the rest of the way or was going to have to walk most of it. But then I remembered the lesson God had been trying to teach me for months. When I first saw, who I would later find out was Rob Dorval, coming towards me to help I knew he was sent to help me and that I would miss out on knowing who this kind man was if I didn't say "yes." So, after asking if he was sure that he was okay with me slowing him down I accepted his offer to finish the race together.

As we walked and talked I wondered if he knew how much of a Godsend he was to me right when I needed it. Each time I would stop to get sick he would wait patiently for me to get ready to stand back up and then offer me his arm to hold as long as I needed. I couldn't believe that someone would be so selfless to do this for a complete stranger. It's not very often especially in a race when people think of others before they think of themselves. After all there were thousands of others who ran right past me without a bat of an eyelash. This is why I was even luckier to have met Rob Dorval that day and have the blessing to have him by my side for those last six miles. It would have been easy for him to just pass me by as I was getting sick on the side of the road, but instead he said he was going to stay with me to make sure I was okay. We were going to cross the finish line together and together we did. Those 26.2 miles taught me more than I would have imagined that day.

As we started to walk I told him more about why I was running. I'm sure it helped him understand why I was so adamant about finishing the race when he saw the T-Shirt my friend had designed for me to wear. It had a photo of my dad and my Uncle Dan with me in the middle when I was ten years old. Above the photo it said, "Happy Birthday", and below, "Always in My Heart." On the backside of the T-Shirt it had a pair of Angel wings with the miles listed for others' loved ones I was running for listed with "My Daddy – Dave Montgomery" under mile 26. I soon found I had to push my pride aside to recognize the true gift that was in front of me in the form of an Earth Angel from Canada. God amazes me how he puts the right people with the right lessons for us to learn along our path. I'm glad I went against my initial reaction of not accepting his help and instead stood up, took his arm that he offered to me like a true gentleman would, and carried on with him instead of being tired, sick and alone. When Rob shared with me that he had been having his own setbacks on the trail with back spasms, I thought to myself, "See Angie, sometimes we help save others just as much as they help save us." Maybe we were sent to each other to support each other that day. If one of us wasn't willing to answer that call we could have had a different outcome.

Suffice it to say the marathon ended up being more challenging than I thought with getting sick along the trail, but one thing was clear I didn't want it to go any other way. I learned so many life lessons along that 26.2 miles that I never would have learned if it would have been an easy run where I finished in my goal time like I trained for. Instead I got multiple gifts along the way. I learned a lot about the human spirit that day, and about the kindness of strangers. I learned I will never give up on my dreams, that life is better when we let people help us even if we think we can do it on our own, that we might be helping others by letting them help us and that God will always put the right person in front of us it's just up to us to see it.

Rob later wrote his account of the day on a photo of us I had uploaded to Facebook, which he told me I could share here. Rob said he had grown to realize that a relationship between a father and daughter is one of a kind as he had a daughter himself. He felt we had met for a reason and had thought to himself if his daughter needed a helping hand he wishes someone would be kind enough to help her. He told me that when he gave me his arm for support, it was as any father would do for his daughter and that he was sure my dad would have done it if he could have. I believe we met for a reason, too. As Rob and I talked towards the end of the run, before our last mile, we both felt my dad was with us that day. Rob said, "There are three of us on this trail, not just two." As we stopped for me to get sick for what would be the last time, I took a moment to pray to God that I would be able to finish the last mile of the run feeling better. I prayed to enjoy this last mile, the one I set aside for my dad. My prayer was answered as Rob and I were able to run the last mile home. I'll never forget Rob reaching back to take my hand in his raising them high above our heads in time for us to cross the finish line together just as he promised me we would. Rob renewed my faith in others by being my Angel for the day.

All the people who supported me, the money I raised towards diabetes research in memory of my dad, and the new friend I met in Rob Dorval were beyond my wildest expectations. And to have achieved all of this in such a short amount of time told me that our spirit can accomplish anything we put our heart to. Even as I was in the midst of finishing the run, I thought to myself, God sure has a way of giving me stories to write in my book. There was just no way He wasn't intentionally giving me more material. I mean really how boring would it have been to have things go smoothly and me finish at the pace I had been training? It made me realize that's what God does. He sets us up for our purpose through our experiences, piece by piece. This experience will remain priceless to me. It's a good illustration to share about the power of reaching for our dreams and seeing them through to the end even when everything in us says we can't take one more step. It taught me that I may need to take a moment to stop and recuperate along the path God puts me on, but that I will never give up on myself or on a friend that chooses to be by my side during times that look and feel difficult. It also taught me that there are souls out there that are meant to find each other and help each other down the road they're walking on. It doesn't matter if you're amongst 50,000 plus runners in the largest city in America, they'll find each other if they're meant to. What got me to that finish line was thinking about how far I'd come along my journey and that I was doing it for my dad. Again, we get to choose how we allow our pain and unhealed hearts to show up in our lives. I chose to allow mine to live and breathe that day. The day ended up very different than I had imagined. It was about meeting someone along my path who embraced the pain I'd been through and helped me turn it into something positive. All the pain, sadness and tears melted like dew drops of sweat dripping from my body with each pound of the pavement. I carried my dad with me that day. Or, rather, he carried me, helping me to step over that finish line. Success is not about crossing a finish line, it's about what happens along the way.

One of the valuable lessons I've learned about grief is that we all grieve differently. We may even be grieving the same person, but that doesn't mean we will react the same way. It is helpful to recognize the way grief shows up in those we are close with may look different than how it shows up for us. Take my little brother, Mikey, for example. He proposed to his girlfriend about six months after our dad passed away. They were married a little over a year later. For him he knew he wanted to be with her forever and there was no sense in waiting. Losing my dad had shown him how short life really is and he wanted to marry his best friend from our hometown. As a way of remembering my dad he was bound and determined to finish refurbishing a classic car of my dads that they had been working on together before my dad passed. The effort and labor of love my brother put into making that 1965 Ford Falcon come alive made my heart swell with pride. Finishing the car they worked on together and every car show he's entered it into since bringing it back to life is an extension of my brothers love. I could see the way my brother was grieving may have looked different than mine, but that we were each finding our way back again. My sissy, Allison, on the other hand had four children to care for at the time and I could gradually see the way losing our dad was shaping her parenting. She would tell the kids stories and make sure they would remember their papa who was an extension of them and all of us. I loved watching my sister keep our dad's traditions alive with her kids like flying kites on Easter Sunday or playing tickle monster with them like my dad would do. We were each keeping my dad alive whether it be refurbishing a car, keeping traditions alive or running in the New York City Marathon. Each was equally special and unique to our own grieving process. And each was an outlet for our pain.

Left to Right: Me, my Mom holding my brother Mike, my sister Allison and my Dad on Easter Sunday.

Left to Right: My Uncle Dan, Me and my Dad enjoying a laugh together.

Left to Right: Me and my beloved Grandma Alice.

Left to Right: My Grandma Margaret and Grandpa Lyle Montgomery set a great example for our family.

Left to Right - Uncle Dan and Uncle Steve in their younger years.

Left to Right - Me and my Dad at the carnival enjoying one of our favorite events together.

Left to Right - My Dad and Uncle Dan when I threw them in "jail" at the carnival.

My Sister's Family. Left to Right - Bottom Row: Annabelle, Madison, Maddox, Landon Top Row: Nate, Leo, Austin, Allison.

Left to Right - My brother Mike holding his baby Myles with his wife Wendy.

My Dad's 1965 Ford Falcon my brother finished restoring.

Left to Right - Me and Shari in the plane before our skydive.

Skydiving with my instructor.

Left to Right - Me and Rob crossing the New York City Marathon finish line.

Me showing the "Angels" I was running for on the back of my
T-shirt after crossing the NYC Marathon finish line.

During my time at the Ashram for my 33rd birthday.

Left to Right - Me and my Nephew Landon the day my sister surprised me in Denver at the park on our Dad's birthday.

Left to Right: My Sister, my Mom, Me and my Brother on my sister's birthday.

Happy to be a Nebraska girl!

Me and Luke. Photo by Jeanne Raises.

Chapter Seven

Kick F-E-A-R to the C-U-R-B

"Dearest Fear: Creativity and I are about to go on a road trip together."
- Elizabeth Gilbert

Become friends with your fear. It's ultimately up to us what we choose to feed it. When we feed fear our dreams it is most likely fear will chew them up and spit them out. Be careful what you decide to feed your fear. I most often like to tell mine to take a hike, but over the years I've learned that the best thing I can feed my fear is love. Because love is the only thing that has the power to transform our fear. When we feed our fear compassion, love and give it a moment of attention it will calm down because like an obnoxious adolescent it just wants to know it's been heard. Once fear feels sufficiently noticed it will take a back seat for our truest journey to begin. In essence, each time we transcend fear we choose love.

There's not a moment in this life that we don't have something important to contribute. Thinking we aren't good enough, not ready, too old, too young, etc. is a bunch of baloney. Those are just passing thoughts, fears, untruths. Forget about that crud and get on with what you're here to do. To be able to say, "I lived", that's where it's at. Live despite the fear and you will have let love win.

Maybe we came here to learn how not to be afraid. To learn to look our biggest fears in the face and say you're not going to get me. I am not going to succumb to the fear that rises to meet me, that rises to steal my joy, that rises to stop me in my tracks. If losing my dad taught me anything it was to not let fear run the show, but instead use it as a tool to do the things in life you want to do. You see if we can learn to master our fear, which does not mean to rid ourselves of fear, but instead to join forces with our fear, welcome it into our lives like an old college friend, to embrace the fear, then the fear is useful. If we let fear get on the catwalk and run the show then we have died to our fear. Fear is a four-letter word for a reason and it can be ruthless. Instead give fear a little run for its money, push back and explain to fear that you can work in conjunction with one another, but not at the sake of one another. We need to learn to dismantle the mystique around fear. Fear can be a great tool in our arsenal to get stuff done.

When I partner with fear in a healthy way I'm able to use it to my advantage and, therefore, take advantage of it instead of it taking advantage of me. There's a giant difference in that last statement. When I use it, it helps guide me to what is important in my life by the fear I feel towards the things that matter. All the fear shows me is that I'm on to something that matters. When it uses me, it catapults me into a place where I get stuck by the lies that fear puts in my head. When we can take fear, and have it work for us it will take us places we've always dreamed of going. The important thing here is to keep fear in check. Remember you run the show and control how big fear gets. Fear has a big ego so be careful not to feed it too much. Fear allows us to determine what is important to us, what we don't want to let slip by and what we want to experience in this life. The more fear I have surrounding something the chances are its significance for me is huge. It's like a barometer showing me the scale of importance. Work with your fear instead of against it. Use the fear to get engaged with what is important in your life.

Although I talk about the things that can hold us back in life this book is much more about conquering the fear. The biggest and brightest message I want to send is one of unfailing hope to keep going for it. No matter what. I'm not going to pretend to know everything you've faced in your life; all the good along with the challenges. But what I do know in my heart is that we are all more alike than we are different. With this understanding, I can tell you with certainty that we have all felt the sting of disappointment, the challenges that inevitably come along with dreams, the rawness of losing something dear to our very existence. These experiences may very easily cause us to stop in our tracks becoming complacent to the matters of our own lives. But what my life has been about is getting back up and taking the next step no matter how seemingly insignificant or small. It's in the small steps that our life evolves, not in the wide leaps that get us where we dream to go. It's the small, steady, patient moments of small movement that catapult us to our destiny. I want you to know you are capable and you are needed in this world. The world needs what only you have to offer. Offer it up like a blessing in your hands, like stardust, leaving it wide open to the Universe to take it where it may. Wrestle with your demons, own up to them, do not let them define who you are or your future. It's all about the perspective we bring to our fears that count. When we free up our egos to believe that these doubts are just that, we recognize they possess no power to hold us back from living our truest destiny and most authentic life.

If you never learn how to jump, how will you reach for the stars?

Along my quest to shake fear off I came across another adventure in the summer of 2012 on a hot July day. I decided along with a few other friends, including my soul sister Shari Suelter and her husband Tim, that it was time for a true adventure. We were all going to take the trek up to 13,000 plus feet in the air and tandem jump out of a plane. It was funny how it worked out. I was at home one night perusing the internet and came across a short video showing skydivers jumping out of a perfectly good plane and decided on a whim I was going to sign up for a redemption boogie taking place a few months later. After talking about it with Shari, I learned that her and Tim, were signing up, too. We all decided to go in on it together. We then talked several other co-workers into doing it, too. It was extremely hot the day of the jump with it being mid-July in Nebraska.

As we arrived we took turns waiting to get geared up for the jump of our lives. Once it was time to board the plane I was more than ready for this adventure. There was something in the air during that time of my life that I had never felt before. It must have been the desire to live and experience life that kept the fear at bay, but when I say I felt no fear, I literally was not scared. I was excited, but not afraid. Looking back, I remember how calm I felt knowing that once again I felt my dad with me. I had this peacefulness within knowing that, "today just isn't my day to go." I felt such peace knowing this was an experience that I was going to be given, almost like a free pass from the Universe allowing me to do something risky.

As the plane began to make its climb to over 13,000 feet above the Earth I just took it all in. I had Shari to my left and Tim across from us. Life just felt right. It's funny how God puts people along our path to experience new adventures with. We were told that once we were high enough up in the air we would need to get in position for our instructor to strap us to them. I ended up with a lighthearted and funny instructor who loved to tease. I could see through his quick wit to the real reason he kept things light. He didn't want the person he was jumping with to get nervous, he tried to keep their attention off what they were doing so they could enjoy the ride. Once again, I found my way to the perfect person. He had shared his story with me, that only over a year before he had gotten in a bad skydiving accident where his parachute hadn't been pulled fast enough, landing him in the hospital for months where he could have easily died from the severity of his injuries. Yet here he was back at it again. I found myself feeling more secure knowing he was my tandem partner. Here God was lining me up with someone who instead of taking the easy road and giving up on his passion, overcame the obstacles. I was getting the blessing of his bravery by being able to jump with him. Once I saw everyone getting safely harnessed to their instructor, I knew it was close to "go time." My friend Shari was the first brave soul to jump out of the plane with me following suit. As we got closer to the edge of the plane my instructor counted down. Once he said "jump" we quickly did a flip outside of the plane. The feeling of the cold air hitting my skin while free falling for the next 8,000 feet was nothing like I'd ever experienced before. All I could do was smile the widest smile of my life while the adrenaline raced through my veins. I felt happy to be so far above the Earth with nothing around me except clouds and sunshine. I felt weightless and free.

Once the parachute was opened at around 5,000 feet the most peaceful feeling swept over my soul. As we floated back down to Earth I became still and silent. I couldn't help but look at life from a different vantage point. I could see for miles and miles. I thought to myself, this is peace, this is what birds must feel. As I took in my final moments in the air, gliding back down to Earth, I felt closer to God and my dad than I had before. It was amazing to think about the view of life from up above when you can see all the pieces of life interconnecting. As we began our descent down to the ground I was instructed to lift my legs to come in for the landing. As we slid in hard along our bottoms all I could think is, "let's do it again, now please!" Shari was waiting for me and came running over to give me the biggest hug. We had done this together like so many other things that we didn't even know were in front of us. We answered the call of our hearts to be free that day. And free we were.

There is nothing brave about listening to our fears.

If we would have allowed fear to overtake us that day we wouldn't have had that experience to reflect on for years to come. Those moments of bravery live in us forever. Those are the moments that call us home to ourselves. Once you know just how brave you are it's hard to ever step back in to anything less. The most important thing that I've learned about life is that we all long to experience it. That's what we all really want is to experience life. Not just survive it, but experience the things in life that are the most exciting for us. The things that make us come alive to ourselves. This is how I felt during the New York City marathon, as I looked around and realized I wasn't just watching someone else do it, I was the one living it. This was how I felt during the skydive, there was that feeling of accomplishment that only comes after doing something that requires overcoming your fears. When it would be easier to shrink back and let life pass you by, but instead you stood up and stood out. Those are the moments we should all strive for. What are your stand out moments? Relish in them. Share them. Live them out loud. Remembering that fear is only our internal detective pointing us in the direction of our biggest desires.

What has helped me during times that I get caught up in fear is to call upon my Angels, crossed over loved ones and spirit guides to lead me to my path of least resistance. They are like our SWAT team coming in to provide us with emergency assistance whenever needed. Instead of letting fear get the best of us we should rely on our team of spiritual beings to bring out the best in us. The great thing is they are readily willing and available to be called upon in a pinch without a moment's notice. They are brought to us as their "assignment" to assist us in reaching our purpose and potential. They want us to call upon them when we need them the most and even during times when things are running smoothly. They delight in seeing us live our lives to the fullest and in turn we help them live vicariously through us. Every adventure I've been on I have no doubt my team of spiritual beings are right there enjoying the ride right along with me. There's even been times I've wondered if they were the ones who were putting some of these wild ideas in my head. Either way they are with us and they are honored when we call on them for assistance. However, being that we are given free choice they are respectful of boundaries and won't step in to interfere with our lives unless we ask for help and give them permission to assist us. My life has become far richer with the inclusion of working with my Heavenly team. I feel surrounded and guided on my path more now than I ever have. I don't feel as alone knowing they are always by my side. Truly what's to be afraid of when you know you have that kind of support in completing your souls mission? We can either choose to live in fear or not. Either way we are going to live and either way we are going to die. My skydive taught me that if we are going to be afraid of anything, we should not be afraid of dying, we should be afraid of not living while we're here.

Chapter Eight

Wild Little Thing

I lose my balance on these eggshells
You tell me to tread, I'd rather be a wild one instead
Then leave us alone, cause we don't need your policies
Find me where the wild things are
We will carve our place into time and space
We will find our way, or we'll make a way
Find you're great, don't hide your face
Let it shine, shine, shine, shine, shine, shine
-Alessia Cara

As I entered 2014 something had changed inside of me. I found myself searching once again for something different. Something that would take me down my path towards learning what true faith is. The last few years had been filled with chasing after my dreams, running towards my next adventure and now as the new year began I noticed that there was something wanting to give birth through me once again. As those first few months of the new year began to pass I realized that the longing came from wanting to experience life in a different city. One I knew nothing about, one I longed to explore. No matter how hard I tried I couldn't shake the feeling that God was trying to guide me some place new and unfamiliar.

I had always had an affinity for Colorado. The first time I crossed the state line from Nebraska to Colorado back in August of 2013 tears welled up in my eyes feeling like I had found another piece of myself. Colorado felt like home. As I reminisced about my time in Colorado the year before I had no idea I would potentially become a resident a short while later. That first trip to Colorado left me feeling love struck with its magical beauty. I had never seen mountains before, witnessing them for the first time as I drove towards my five-day birthday retreat winding my way through the Flatirons, I would never have imagined the significance they would play in my spiritual quest to find more and more moments alone with God. Colorado was beautiful. The moment I saw it the colors stood out to me in a way I had never imagined. The majestic sunrises of various shades of orange and pink lifted my spirits and showed me God does exist within the sky. Even when it's just an ordinary day in Colorado there is something beautiful to see with the bright yellow sun shining down upon your face and into your heart. It's as if my heart belonged there and knew deep down that was exactly where I longed to be. The lush green pine trees outlining the streets and the mountains with rocks of varying shades of brown and grey captured my heart. I love the earth tones that surround Colorado making me feel calm. I loved the bright blue skies and the lakes that would pop up in the most unexpected of places and spaces. Colorado is full of the unexpected. You turn one corner to something completely different than the one that you left behind. Needless to say, I was in love.

During my first trip to Colorado, as I finally arrived at my destination, I made my way to park in front of the Ashram's office to check in to my cabin. I couldn't believe the absolute peace that surrounded me. It was the cutest place. As I pulled in I saw cabins sprinkled around the office with a temple at the end of the drive. As I checked in and settled into my cabin, I found there were so many ways to explore who I was. I had long been drawn towards Yoga, meditation and the Buddhist philosophy. Being in an environment where all I had to do for five days straight was attend as many yoga classes as I wanted, spend time writing in my journal, go to meditation circles and on hikes to explore the land felt magical to me. Those five days proved to be just what I needed. There was nothing to do other than be one with nature. No cell service felt freeing to me that week.

I woke up early in the morning in the wee hours on my birthday to attend a fire ceremony at 4:30 a.m. followed by a meditation class. I started off my morning right. Before showering and throwing on the yoga dress I had purchased in the shop at the retreat the day before I put a single candle in the cupcake I had brought with me from home. As I hovered over the lit candle singing happy birthday to myself I couldn't help but close my eyes and smile at the adventure I had made of my life. As I blew out the candle I soaked in the gift my journey was turning out to be. I was at a point in my life where being at a yoga retreat by myself in the mountains was something I was relishing in. I wanted to ring in the fresh new year on my own. I think we should all spend at least one birthday doing something for ourselves. Being able to sit with yourself and feel at complete peace is a gift unto itself. As I rushed to get ready and out the door to make the fire ceremony I was filled with excitement to embark upon another year. One that, once again like all the others, I had ideas of what I would like it to show me, but knew inevitably there would be more twists and turns along the way.

As I stepped out the door of my cabin and descended upon the stairs to run my way over to the temple I looked up at the early morning sky, being so high in the mountains, it was like you could see every star for all its true beauty. I looked up at the sky and thanked God for bringing me here. Not just to this moment at the Ashram, but to this life He's given me. Over the course of those next few days I met extraordinary human beings who were just as in sync with their own journeys. The delicious vegan meals that we shared as a community while sitting outside on a sprawling deck made me feel at home. I made my way outside to the hot tub my final night at the retreat to take in the full moon. As I sat alone soaking up the warmth from the hot tub I couldn't imagine wanting to be any place other than where I was. I looked up at the full moon and made a wish knowing it would listen. I asked it to teach me all that it had to show me. The waxing and the waning of life is embodied within the moon and its wisdom. As I made the trek down the mountain the next day to begin the journey home I was filled with a sense of wonder that the mountains are a magical place indeed. I had hiked and climbed my way to one of the highest points around the Ashram to meditate at the top looking out over God's green Earth. I had risen early to watch the breaktaking Colorado sunrise show me its beautiful colors of orange and yellow. I had once again found God during the quiet and the stillness that only the mountains can bring. I was leaving having found another piece of myself.

A year later as I was feeling my way towards relocating, my heart thought back to my time in Colorado. I loved the Ashram and what I had seen of Boulder just as much. Everything about that solo soul trip felt sacred to me. I began to feel a tug at my heart leading me to my next adventure. At the time I had taken my first trip there I had no idea I would potentially become a resident a short while later. I was almost surprising myself at my desire to move. I loved living around my family, my job was stable, I had been working there for twelve years and had recently become the Human Resources Director working my way towards this accomplishment for years. Yet there was something missing. Something I couldn't quite put my finger on. For several years I had longed to go into business for myself as a life coach. There were so many things I had yet to check off my "dream" list and I figured this was as good of a time as any to follow this next set of dreams. I thought if I was going to take the plunge and move it would be smart to do it now while I was still young and unattached.

As the feeling continued to persist I took the opportunity in September of 2014 to go look at apartments outside of Boulder to see if this was truly where I could see myself living. During my trip, I visited several potential apartment complexes. When I visited the final apartment of the trip it sang to my heart. The day before I met with the office at the apartment, I stood outside of the complex and prayed to the Lord that if this was meant for me they would have a two-bedroom apartment overlooking the Flatirons for me to house my life coaching business out of. The next day, lo and behold, that was exactly what they had open. It took me about twenty-four hours to decide this is what I wanted to do. I felt called to this new destination. I put my deposit on the apartment and went back to Omaha to take the next month and a half to finalize my plans and continue to job search in the Denver/Boulder area. I had been working with recruitment firms and applying for jobs in the area online here and there for months to no avail. After talking with several people about the job market in Denver it was suggested that I move to the area and continue my search as most employers in the area are going to be more serious about hiring someone if they are local and this was a common practice in the area for people to relocate without finding work first.

Since I had managed to save up enough to get me by until I found work I decided I was just going to have to take the leap and in the meantime while looking for work I could build my life coaching business in my free time. The time seemed to fly by since I'd returned from finding my new apartment and before I knew it, it was time to spread my wings and fly. I have been so blessed in my life to be surrounded by family who supports me. My brother, Mike, has been one of my constant supporters. Although he's six years younger than me and I will always consider him my little brother, since my dad passed away he took the lead role of the man in my family. He's always been there to help me when I need it and moving to Colorado was one of those times. My brother Mike, cousin Tony, and my dear friend Janette loaded up my U-Haul and we headed West towards my new home.

I had been so excited about the move that it caught me off guard when I felt my stomach drop crossing the Colorado State Line. I remember telling Janette, "I don't know why but suddenly my stomach hurts like it's full of anxiety." I chalked it up to nerves and went about the business of being excited. After we arrived we spent the majority of that evening unpacking and getting my things all settled in as my moving crew would be heading home first thing in the morning. As morning came and I bid my farewells, I couldn't understand this deep feeling inside that I just wanted to go home with them. Here I was in my new home and yet I couldn't imagine living here. I'll never forget the gut wrenching feeling of waking up in Colorado the first morning on my own without any of my security blankets to comfort me. It was that feeling in the pit of my stomach coming back again only this time asking me in a somewhat hysterical voice what I had just done to my life. In much the same way, we wake up in a panic after a long nightmare, but only this time it was my new reality. I instantly thought to myself that this must just be the way you feel when you do something new you've never done before. I sure didn't want to be trapped by fear so soon into my move. Yet fear had me captured at its door. As the weeks went by in my new home I found that I was once again feeling deep grief over the life I had just left behind. I missed my job and my co-workers many of whom had supported me from the time I was in my early twenties. Even that paled in comparison to the grief I felt over not being able to see my family whenever I wanted. But here I was on the other side of the move and I was going to have to keep moving along to see what exactly it was that made me feel like God wanted me here.

I would venture to guess that not many people have done what I did. Leaving it all behind to go on a spiritual journey alone with God not knowing a single soul. I may not have realized it at the time, but that was exactly what I was getting myself into when I left Nebraska. I was asking Spirit to lead me to Him. To learn more about another way of life. One that I had longed to know. For my life to unfold I had to understand what it felt like to live somewhere that you couldn't even get around without looking at your GPS. Along that journey I did find more of myself. I found the part of her that could no longer run herself ragged with the day to day distractions of life. There was too much silence for that now. Instead of running from her, thinking I had to somehow evolve in to being someone else, I finally accepted who I've always been and who I will always be. What parts of yourself are you running from? To embrace the pieces of ourselves that aren't always happy, fun and shiny, to integrate them into our everyday lives as part of the human experience is crucial to our health and wellbeing. To not embrace parts of who we are causes us to fight the negative feelings we experience even more. We don't like to sit with our negative emotions because they cause us pain and discomfort.

This form of avoidance leaves us running from ourselves when what we need to do is sit with our multitude of emotions and feel them to move beyond them. This is one of the reasons why finding a form of meditation, quiet reflection, or prayer is important. If we can learn to embrace the feelings we want to avoid and instead sit with them this will help us resolve them faster by moving through them. We will feel these feelings whether we avoid them or embrace them. Part of finding yourself is finding what works for you. Explore yourself, your feelings, your options surrounding what you believe in. Part of living an authentic life is giving yourself the permission to pursue life on your terms. Finding what you believe in is a freeing experience and will open doors you never dreamed possible.

Learning is a part of evolving and becoming more of who you truly are. The more you learn the more you're given to learn. Remember you came to dance with life, to play with it, and to relish in the mere fact that you're alive. You're here now. There is a reason you're here. There's a purpose to your existence. Nothing and no one is an accident. You may not have all the answers, but why would you want to? That would mean there's nothing left to explore and that would lead to a very mundane existence. My time in Colorado left me with nothing else to do, but explore. My time being freed up led me to joining MeetUp groups trying to get my life coaching business off the ground, but more importantly gave me an opportunity to meet new friends. Even though the days were long and the nights even longer I realized that the mountains were making me long for the Nebraska plains once again. I missed not being able to run for miles at a time without much of an issue. I was having a hard time getting used to life at this altitude. When you're in a place of feeling hopeless, desperate, confused and frankly like you want to give up, pack it up, go back home and never face the outside world again is when you probably shouldn't throw in the towel just yet. You might miss out on the miracle that is waiting for you if you would only take a few more steps forward.

My move to Colorado felt like it took the wind out of my sails. I was having such a hard time settling in that I wondered if I'd made a huge mistake. And for someone who was full of energy and optimism those were difficult emotions to accept. We all have those moments in our lives that try us, challenge everything we believed in and thought was possible for our lives. And therein lies the choice. We can either rise from those broken dreams we find ourselves in or we can settle for less of a life than the one we know is still out there. The one that we still deserve and that is meant for us. The thing we must learn is just because we go through something difficult does not mean that our destiny is still not right on track. The timing you thought it would happen in may be off, you may have more learning to do along the path, but you're still headed in the direction of your calling.

Under the pain, the confusion, and the doubt your knowing should remain the same. This can be one of the hardest parts of the journey.

Our mind wants to tell us to throw in the towel when things get tough, that we made a misstep and yet our intuition, our heart and our knowing tells us an entirely different story. During this time, we must listen to this knowing. If there is something in life that you feel and believe deeply that you are meant to do with your talents you have to try. But don't just stop at try. You have to keep going when the road you began traveling down gets bumpy and your mind wants to tell you to give up on your dream, which in turn is giving up on yourself. Please do not listen to those voices in your head. They may consume you for a time, but when you gain back your strength and stamina you must return to the game of life once again. The game you set out to play, the game you find worth playing for. Those voices in your head, the ones that sound more like resignation and defeat, those voices are not your friend, they will lead you astray. Separate yourself from those voices as soon as possible. They want to be heard, agreed with, and listened to. It's our jobs to not do this to ourselves. Do what you must do to change those voices to positive ones instead of giving in to them.

"Because you know that the testing of your faith produces perseverance."
James 1:3

My move to Colorado taught me a lot about having a dream and being disappointed about the outcome. As I literally watched my dream of loving Colorado go up in smoke it was difficult to understand why my dream wasn't panning out the way I had envisioned it in my heart. To put it mildly, I was broken hearted, devastated and plain fed up with the outcome of the decision to move. My expectations about what the move would create in my life were not realistic. Since I had never moved away from home before I didn't know what I should expect. First time learning is usually the hardest. I couldn't understand why God had put this dream in my heart just to find out once I took one of the biggest leaps of faith of my life how wrong it felt to make the decision to uproot my life and follow a new path. I had always secretly dreamed to experience life in a new place from a new vantage point. I couldn't possibly understand why

I felt so strongly that I was being guided to take this adventure when it felt so hard. I couldn't possibly understand why if I really was listening to God Himself that this was turning out to feel more like a nightmare than a dream. It took me months to realize that there are times in life when God will allow us to go down a path and the lessons we learn are hard for us, but in the long run they are beneficial for our future. When you ask God to be on this path there is a misconception that it will be easy and we will walk down roads paved of gold. When that doesn't happen, we think we missed the mark, as if we got off course and we begin to second guess everything we thought we knew. It shakes our confidence and makes us fearful to make brave decisions again in the future.

But then as I dug deeper I started to learn more about God. I was growing closer to Him in a new and different way. After being in Colorado for a few months I began to realize that God did call me to move there. Before the move I had prayed for time alone with God to really understand who He was without any distractions. My Colorado time was allowing just that, I was growing closer to God in every way because I literally had to rely on Him just to get by. Every morning when I woke up, I'd ask God what it was we were going to do today. With a pretty open schedule and still searching for work, I would let Him lead my day. Sometimes it would consist of working all day from morning until night on my life coaching business, attending MeetUp groups and going to interviews. Other times it would be spending time with some new girlfriends I had found along my path. All of which were a true blessing.

This time in my life brought me no other choice, but to experience patience. When you are at a point where things are not moving along in the timing of your own will you learn that if you want to get through the drought season you better build up enough patience to make it to the other side where abundance, hope and movement live. I felt stuck. Stuck like a rain boot in the wet sloppy mud. Have you ever felt stuck? I did from the inside out. It was tempting to just give in, to stop going for it. But giving in felt too much like giving up for my heart to handle. God made us full of heart, no wonder it hurts so much when the very things we love the most are ripped away from us causing us to suffer. It's easy to write uplifting words about suffering. It's much harder to live those words. But there are gifts in everything. Through the hard, stuck, immobile, soulless days, I have learned what the good days feel like. The good days usually aren't anything extraordinary unless you count feeling whole an extraordinary day.

These days I count the inner critic being at bay one of the extraordinary days. The days where you feel at peace with your life, your blessings, and your sufferings. The days where fears submerge and wisdom prevails out of the depths of our suffering where we find hope again. Or maybe I'm just doing a better job of exercising my patience these days. Which doesn't mean giving up. It means giving in. Giving in to the plan of all plans. Giving in simply means making a choice to enjoy the journey and trust with all completeness that you can't possibly mess up your destiny. As my soul sister Shari has told me, "How funny to think we could mess up God's plan." Know in your heart of hearts that you'll get there. I tried to get better at enjoying all that was on offer to me right then.

When used correctly patience can be one of our best friends instead of our worst enemies. When we are called to be patient in our lives it opens windows, doors, and complete worlds for us to meander through while we are awaiting our ultimate destination. I mean seriously, isn't that all life really is? A meandering of sorts. I liken it to walking through the forest. There are so many different paths to take, some look more interesting than others, but somehow there is a knowing that no matter which path you take you'll get to your fork in the road. If you veer off the path and take the wrong road the almighty Universe will point you in the right direction to bring you home safely where you belong. Life is like that forest. Much bigger than we'll ever be and full of surprise twists and turns. I suppose life would be much less exciting if the path were already paved.

I'll never forget one weekend morning when I went out for a jog before my move to Colorado. I'd been feeling like my life was calling for me to start the true adventure of why I was here and yet I wasn't sure what it was calling me towards. I had spent the last couple of years pushing myself to try new things and experience life in a new and different way. That day on the trail it felt like the last few years were preparing me to take another giant leap. As I prayed during my run the message that came to me was this, "Being brave is walking down a path even though no one else is on it." Well, that made a lot of sense. No wonder I had a knowing deep inside that I asked for bravery in this life and God always knew just how to dish it up. Maybe I was just asking for it, but somewhere in my soul's knowing I was acutely aware that I would be going off on my own soon to experience what I needed to experience before the next stage of my life would begin. It was in my hands, I still had choices but I had already chosen to follow my true path several years ago. Even if the road frightened me I was not going to compromise my life any longer. I needed to live the life I signed up for and if going it alone was part of the plan by golly I was going to follow it. This was the first day that I knew I would be moving away from home on my own. I didn't know when, where, or how yet. I heard the call and knew I would have to muster the courage to do as I was guided.

It was almost a year later that my U-Haul was packed, loaded and ready to take the 500 plus mile trek to Colorado where I didn't know a soul. But for goodness sake being brave is walking down a path even though no one else is on it and I was dead set on being brave. The thing I learned quickly about truly being brave is it can hurt. It's almost guaranteed that by being brave you will find yourself in some painful situations, but what a way to learn and learn quickly. This next chapter in my life felt like it included an in between time, as if I had to somehow make the trek from point A to point B. For me to fully find my true self I needed to walk over an imaginary bridge to find a lot of gems I was meant to pick up along the way. I think that bridge was my time spent in Colorado with me, myself and I. Little did I know that when I set off on my journey I would return home a changed person. Although relatively short lived, the six-month hiatus to Colorado taught me more about myself than any other move had. It taught me to accept myself for who I am. Being brave led me to shedding parts of myself I no longer needed. We never know what event in our life is going to have the most profound transformation for us. The old must die for the new to be born. The rebirthing process is not an easy one. It takes grit, determination. The energy it calls forth is astounding. Some people aren't ready while others are thrust into situations where there is no choice but to come undone to be redone.

The concept of transformation sounds romantic like something we will have no problem navigating our way through. This is not the kind of transformation I'm talking about. I'm talking about the kind that grips at our soul, asking us to shed the things that no longer serve us for our next journey to begin, the kind where you feel like there are pieces of you that are dying because they are. The pieces you are not going to need anymore.

There are three phases to the transformation process: the deconstruction, the rebirth and the building anew. Deconstruction is a requirement for the transformation process to take place and it's the phase that is the toughest. It's the phase where you're not sure if you will survive the storm that you're in. It's the place that's so dark and so deep you're not sure if you will make it out alive. Sometimes you'll find during this phase that you have a major life change. One you decided to make or one that happens to you. But either way, even if it's of your choosing, there is no doubt there is something greater than you at work in your life. We may anticipate the major life transition going smoother than it does, but it's not meant to. This phase can be filled with utter confusion. You may wonder what is going on with your life. This is a painful yet necessary part of the process. You're not meant to know what is coming next, because if you knew you may not have signed up for the experience in the first place. We don't get from point A to point B without the bumps and bruises we get along the way.

The truth was I really didn't know what I was getting myself into before jumping. Yet here I was and I was determined to make the most of it even when roadblock after roadblock felt like it was falling in my path making it difficult beyond measure to take a step forward. I had no clue that being on God's path was going to mean that I was going to have to be stripped bare of everything that I was to make room for who I was going to become. If I was going to do the spiritual work God assigned for me to do I was going to have to learn to walk in faith.

Early on I realized that faith is easy when things are going well in your life. When you're in a good place it's easy to feel grateful. When you're in the darkest hour, and things seem to be headed in a much different direction than you wanted, it can be much more challenging to find the gratitude.

Up until this point me and fear had walked together occasionally, but by the point that I was living in Colorado I knew fear much more intimately. Always hiding out ready to taunt me. I let it take over my life. It ran wild. I tried to chase it down, beat it over the head and throw it in the trash, but it kept coming at me.

What do we do when we are living in fear? The answer is we must have faith. I had some work to do in this area. And God knew it. He was challenging me to grow stronger in my faith and in my relationship with Him. Instead of seeking out worldly treasures, He was asking me to seek the biggest treasure of all, Him. Our testimony is always being strengthened. I knew if I had faith and believed then I could take steps in the right direction. This was all part of my faith walk. My time in Colorado felt so heavy that it could have led me to becoming a non-believer, but instead through the pain of all the lows I was experiencing I knew it was making me stronger and more than anything else I knew in my heart it wouldn't last forever. This was my faith rising.

Take a moment to ask yourself this question, do you build your faith in the easy times or in the challenging times? I would tend to venture a guess towards the times of struggle and strife. When you decide to partner with God, He is going to test you. It is not going to be a cake walk. I had high hopes that it would be, but then I got a reality check. What kept me moving forward? The same God that put me to the test. You see, your test becomes your testament. You must believe you will get through it. The testimony will come. You will have to be strong, build your endurance and pass the testing period. For you to do great things you will have great challenges. The trial period is for your good. You will be stronger, learn humility, and become an overall better person.

Time in many ways has felt both like a blessing and a curse. Time is something we never feel like we have enough of yet there are times when it is the only thing we know that will heal our broken hearts. Colorado was such a painful experience, yet there were some days that the only thing that got me by was knowing that one day it would get better. I knew this experience wouldn't last forever and that was the hope that I would cling to. When we are in happy places in our lives we don't want time to pass. It's almost as if we think it's going to last forever. We can move forward easily in times of joy, but that becomes much more difficult during times of loss, confusion, and immense pain. When we are going through hard times it feels like there is no light at the end of the tunnel. We can't fathom a way out so we can get drug down by the day to day responsibilities of life. We can feel frightened, terrified and lost, but if we can deeply believe that one-day things will change we can keep going. It's when we let our negative emotions completely control our hope that we run into problems.

"For a seed to achieve its greatest expression, it must come completely undone. The shell cracks, its insides come out and everything changes. To someone who doesn't understand growth, it would look like complete destruction."
-Rumi

After only a few weeks in Colorado, I woke up in the middle of the night, dread gripping my stomach tying it in knots embedded with regret. What had I just done with my life? Crawling out of bed to escape my new reality, hands and knees to the ground, more panic. Fear coming to the surface disguised as heat welling up inside of me. A panic attack. This was all so foreign to me. I'd never had one before and thought it would never end. This would be my life from here on out. I was sure of it. Why couldn't my old life have been enough for me? Why did I have to leave everything I knew and loved back home? For what, for this? I must have made the wrong decision and everything in my body was making sure I knew it. The fear of the unknown that was crippling me felt relentless. I thought my move to Colorado was going to be my Elizabeth Gilbert moment, but so far it was more of a nightmare than an enlightened experience.

I called my dear friend, Andrea, in Seattle who always had a way of comforting me. As always, she came through for me, her coaching skills kicked in and I was able to remember why I felt so strongly about making this huge life change. I quickly remembered the feeling I had on the other side of the move. The one where I felt inspired and like I was going to go kick butt on my new adventure. So why then on this side of the move was I feeling more like life was kicking my butt?

I later learned that we have grief over any big loss in our lives. We don't just grieve the people we lose, we grieve chapters of our lives. The chapter I had just said goodbye to was a significant one that I would always treasure, it was natural that I was experiencing grief in my new city. I wasn't sure how to get back on solid ground with nothing familiar around me. I soon learned, especially in those first few days and weeks, that some days all I could do was inch out of bed in the morning to face my new reality. There was something much bigger at play going on in my life and it wasn't my job to know what it was. Every time I tried to dig deeper into the meaning of all of this I only fell further into the rabbit holes that began to occupy my mind telling me all sorts of dark stories that my mind gladly entertained.

I had time on my hands and nothing much else to fill my time with. Even with going out most days, trying to meet new people, I felt lost. During those times where I didn't think I could go on for another hour, let alone another day, I had to remind myself that God was still there even if I couldn't feel him in my deepest despair. There was some small knowing still inside of me saying, "I'm here, I always will be." I grappled with not understanding why God would allow this situation to enter my life. If He loved me and I felt guided to make this move how in the world was it ending up this way?

Can you relate to this in seasons of your own life? These thoughts I'd never thought before began to flood my mind holding me hostage. But then, as if out of nowhere when I was feeling the most alone, God would send me one of His angels in the form of one of my friends from back home. I'd get a call or a text or a message as a reminder that first and foremost I'm never alone because I have God and secondly my friends were all still there rooting me on from the sidelines. Looking back on it now, one of the things that made this time in my life sweet was experiencing a move at the same time my wonderful friend Shari had. She had up and moved from Nebraska to Portland with her husband Tim a month before my move to Colorado. As we were all settling in and had time on our hands we would spend time on FaceTime supporting one another through this transition. Our talks meant the world to me at a time when I needed every ounce of peace I could get.

There was one evening in particular that stood out to me, Tim, brought up the story of Job in the Bible. Job had a wonderful life and fully believed in God and then difficult things started happening to him like losing his children and becoming ill. Through all his trials he never stopped believing in God and was ultimately rewarded once again by keeping his commitment and being a good steward of his faith. I loved this thought. Isn't it beautiful to know that the God who brings you to it will bring you through it? If the only point of my Colorado time was to grow closer in my faith in God, then it was well worth it, a true gift of a lifetime. God continued to bring people to me right when I needed them.

Take the day my sister showed up to surprise me with two of my nephews out of nowhere. I hadn't been in Colorado for long and it happened to be my dad's birthday once again. It was always hard to have another year go by without being able to celebrate with him. I had recently talked to my mom and brother as they were out celebrating my Uncle Dan's birthday with him. I missed my family and wanted nothing more than to be celebrating with them. While I was on the phone with my mom she asked me where I was. I let her know I was at a park in Denver getting some fresh air since I felt so homesick I figured it would be good to get outside for a bit. I must have been off the phone with my mom for maybe fifteen minutes and decided it was time to head back home. As I started pulling my car out of the parking lot, I just happened to glance over at a mom with two little boys. I couldn't help but think the little boy running my way looked like my little "lovebug", Landon, who was eight years old at the time. I figured I must really be losing my mind. But as they kept walking closer I could make out my sister holding my other nephew Maddox. I've never parked my car so fast in my life. I flung open my car door and ran towards them faster than I'd moved since I got to Colorado. My sister had decided that morning to drive the eight hours to Colorado to spend our dad's birthday together as a surprise. She knew I was having a hard time and seeing them would cheer me up. Boy did it. My sister once again proved to me that the people in our lives are our biggest blessing.

There are many ways to build strength, endurance and agility. Many of these traits come from going through something where you had no other choice, but to be strong. When God gives you mountains to move there is going to have to be some amount of tenacity, endurance, and above all else willingness to keep trekking up those mountains, to be strong and brave enough to sustain yourself during the valleys. During my time alone in Boulder, I felt isolated and alone finding myself grieving once again. Grieving the life that I had, the life that still felt like me, but that no longer existed except in my not too distant memory. I felt like my dream was falling short and the only option I had was to take life day by day. At times, moment by moment. I hadn't bargained for the extreme homesickness I was experiencing and for the first time there was no quick answer in sight. Nothing to take my mind off the decision I had made, but somewhere the ember was still burning in the fire of my soul knowing on a very deep, raw level that I signed up to experience this very situation. God was taking me to new levels of depth and awareness of what living in His will for my life meant.

I began to witness firsthand the utter dissonance between our minds and our hearts and that when we suffer it is in the mind not in the heart. You see the mind is full of nonsense during times of stress and change. It will try to get you to jump down every rabbit hole it can imagine. The heart trusts, knows, feels, and is one of the wisest most loving parts of who we are. The heart believes, the mind challenges. I'll never forget the night I tossed and turned all night wondering what I should do next. I wasn't happy in Colorado yet I was forcing myself to stay there half out of embarrassment and the other half out of sheer will to make this dream I had work out. I remember lying in bed praying to God to help me find peace when I suddenly heard, "You need to learn not to do this to yourself." I inquisitively asked, "What am I doing?", unable to recognize that my own mind was causing my upset. I heard God offering up, "Being too hard on yourself."

Here I was beating myself up for making the decision to move to Colorado not knowing what the experience would be. How could I have known? That's what walking in faith means, to go forth and follow your guidance without being married to an outcome. When we put pressure on ourselves to "know better" we don't allow ourselves the freedom to let go and live the journey. There were undoubtedly lessons I needed to learn, my dark night of the soul to experience and learning to rely on God for all my day to day needs. I felt like a baby in a momma's arms being thrown out into the wilderness to find her way. That's what the dark night of the soul brings up in us. The wilderness and wild parts of our story that only we can find the way out of. It made sense that the way I was going to be thrust in to mine was by being forced to be without all my old crutches. My biggest one being over activity and getting caught up in helping others. Now there was no one else here to help except myself. Now I found myself having to let go of all my old attachments so that something new could be born. It's not easy to let go of relationships, pain, loss, love, a job, or even our dreams. These attachments make up our lives. If someone says you should just let go and move on, look them square in the eyes and tell them you're trying but it's easier said than done. It's just plain not easy to let go of the things that we love. Even the things we think we will be happy to let go of sometimes take us by surprise with the letting go process not being as easy as we had hoped. It's important to remember when letting go that it's a process just like anything else in life and doesn't magically happen overnight. Over time it will become easier to move forward and release some of the attachments we hold onto when all we want is to let go. One thing I know for sure is that it is in the unraveling that we become. We can't hold ourselves down and expect to rise on a whim. The rebirthing process takes time, energy and our ego must allow for it.

> *"God grant me the serenity to accept the things I cannot change, the courage to change the things I can, and the wisdom to know the difference."*
> *- Reinhold Niebuhr*

Maybe God talks to us most in isolation. Not for His benefit, but for ours. He can get through to us the easiest without much interruption. We can't always hear when life is moving right along at a breakneck pace. For some of us it might take a wakeup call, a life changing event, or a down right crisis to get us vulnerable enough to listen to the voice within. During the difficult times in life remember there is always light waiting for you on the other side of the darkness. However you need to get to the light just get there. Don't be hard on yourself, but also don't allow the darkness to settle upon you for too long. Remember life will get easier. Whether you see a way out of your situation in the moment or not there is something waiting for you. Like a breath of fresh air, it will descend upon you when you least expect it and give you a moment of grace. Even in the moments you don't understand why curveballs are thrown your way they are there to teach you and help you grow into the person you've always wanted to become. Let it be what it is. The darkness of it all, it's the dark places we go to within our own souls. Allowing ourselves to go to the parts we aren't proud of, the parts we thought we had released long ago, are the parts that need healing the most. Deep down someplace in the abyss that feels like your life crumbling around you, you know that you will be better for this experience. It may not happen right now and it may not happen for a long time, but the point is, it will happen. You will come back to yourself and the true nature of who you are will emerge once again.

During the toughest times in life you learn what you are truly made of. And it's okay if you want to change course. Don't ever feel like you have to make any decisions except the ones that are best for you. And the truth is there are times you may make a decision and have a tough time with why you made the decision you did, but let that feeling of complete overwhelm and discomfort ascend upon you. Walk through it, lean into it. Remember why it is you made the decision you made. Don't lose sight of why you made the decision in the first place and never give up. If it was an authentic action then you know you did something based in love and light not for the wrong reasons. The road ahead may be a tough one but you wouldn't have taken it if deep down inside you knew you couldn't handle it. God will hold you during your toughest times, He truly is there for you. Letting go is one of the hardest things in the world. If we let go of who we were, then who does that make us now?

The real reason for my journey to Colorado.

I found myself in Colorado, alone and afraid, and rethinking my decision to uproot my life. All of it for what? For this? But then I began finding groups to connect with and would get something out of each connection. One of the MeetUp groups was based in a town outside of Denver for writers to visit with other writers. Part of the session had an allotted amount of time to free flow and write whatever came to our minds. There was a long period of my life where all I did was talk to God. Until one day I realized He talks back. For some reason on that day I started writing to God. I had never done this before so when I started getting responses back, which felt like they were not my own, I was somewhat hesitant to believe it was really Him. But then as I read what I had scribed back to myself I recognized there was something different about the responses He was giving. It sounded and felt different than my own voice. The voice that was talking back was wise, and thoughtful. The truth in the voice began to pierce straight to my heart. Here is an excerpt of that conversation.

Angie: What it is you have for me? I'll turn my doubt and sadness into love for you. I'm sorry I'm mad at you, but I am. I'm mad that I had to come here and be all alone. I'm mad that for some reason you think I can handle more than I feel at times. And I'm mad that I feel this way. I'm angry that I feel so sad. I thought those days were behind me. I'm mad that I have to begin again and I'm mad that I couldn't have just been happy back home. I'm mad. I just want out of this situation. I'm mad that I can't conjure up some gratitude. I'm mad that this is what I wanted and I can't handle it. I'm mad that I feel like I have no one and I know that's not true. I'm mad. I'm mad that things never feel like they're enough to me. I'm mad that I had to move here without a job or income. I'm mad that I'm scared. I'm mad that I feel desperate and weak and like a disappointment. I'm mad that I can't adjust as easily as others. I'm mad that I can't get rid of this dread and doom that I feel. I'm mad that I have to come up with my own answers. I'm just mad. I'm mad at life. That nothing has turned out the way I had planned. I'm mad that I'm thirty-four and I'm alone because I can't let someone in. I'm mad that I try and I feel like I spin my wheels and end up in the same old pitiful place.

I'm mad. Are you there, do you hear me?

Under it all though I'm sad. Like so sad. I have had a huge loss and I don't know how to deal with it. I don't know when the sun is going to come again. I'm scared to be alone. I thought I was doing good and now I'm smack dab in the middle of the depths again.

I'm mad that I don't know what is next. That I don't have any bearings. I'm mad that I don't know if I really want to be here.

Now please with a level head and an open heart help me. Give me peace and calm during this storm I am in. This is not easy for me. And I don't know how to get myself out of it and I need You now. I want to feel You, to breathe You in and experience You. I need to know You are there. That You are beside me, in me, loving me and giving me what I need in every moment. I'm sorry I don't know how to trust yet. I'm sorry I don't know how to just simply be yet. But I'm working on it.

Even in this dark time in my life I still want to write for You and be Your sunshine. Right now, I just don't know how. I got lost in it. I got lost in the emotions of it all. I wasn't sure I wanted it anymore, but I do. I just don't want to continue to experience this change the way I have been for the last week. But I also can't fight the feelings of grief I've been experiencing. I must grieve the girl I was to make room for the woman I'm becoming. The one who was strong enough to choose a life she wanted instead of the one that was handed to her. The truth about Omaha – to gain some perspective – is that I wasn't happy there, was I? What I had was as good as it was going to get and it just never felt quite like me, but this doesn't either. I need to learn not to do this to myself like You said when I heard You tell me to stop being hard on myself. Can You help me, God, to understand what it is I need to stop doing? And what I can do in the moment to stop doing it?

God: Stop losing faith, stop overthinking, stop letting fear get the best of you, stop letting your emotions run wild.

Angie: What do I do instead? How do I stop this from happening?

God: Take control, ask me for help, go for a walk, take deep breaths, keep yourself busy.

Angie: God, will I ever be happy again?

God: Of course, my little sunshine.

Angie: Lord, here is the big one, the big question. Did I make the right decision in moving to Colorado?

God: Without a doubt.

Angie: Ok then. Enough of second guessing. Onward.

Will You help me let go later? Will You please be there with me when I go up into Boulder after this and let go of my Omaha?

God: I always have been there and I always will be.

Angie: Will You help me to do it, the letting go of it all because I don't know how?

God: You do know how, you just don't want to do it. It makes you afraid that you won't know who you are if you let go or you're more afraid of who you will become, but, little girl, you will always be you. Just a lighter you. You don't have to carry the weight of the world and other people's problems like they're your own. I want you to be free. You're not going anywhere you will always be you.

Angie: Lord, can I do this?

God: Of course, you can.

Angie: Lord, am I going to have a mini meltdown again? Like the panic attacks again?

God: No, those are behind you.

Angie: Lord, I'm scared I'm going to break and never come back is that even true?

God: No, you're strong and you're not going to break Angie. You're fine. This is just part of what you need to go through. You're learning. It doesn't have to be like this, you are making it harder on yourself than you need to. Its okay, things haven't worked out the way you wanted them to, you need to let that go.

Angie: Is there a plan for my life?

God: Yes, and you are on it. You have a beautiful heart and you take things hard because you love people so much.

Angie: Lord, is there a guy waiting for me.

God: Yes, and I will reveal him to you when the time is right.

I then began to ask God deeper questions to life. I'd already known for a few years that my purpose was to be a writer, life coach, and motivational speaker. God had answered my call when I had been out running on the trail a few years earlier in 2012 during a time when I knew it was time to fully turn my life over to Him. During that fateful day on the trail I asked God what it was He brought me to Earth for and He answered. It was the day my life changed forever. Now it was clear He was putting me to the test while sharing some of what He wanted me to tell His people in this book.

Angie: Lord, I just need to live in the moment more, huh?

God: Exactly, otherwise you get too wound up. That's not good for you. Don't think past today. There is no need to. I don't expect you to have everything figured out. I just want you to enjoy your experience and what I am trying to give you. You are not alone. I don't want you to struggle.

Angie: Lord, why do I struggle so much? Is there something wrong with me?

God: No, there is not something wrong with you. You struggle because you care. Because you so desperately want to be the best you can be, but the thing is you are so wonderful just the way you are. I want you to stop being hard on yourself and just be okay. You don't have to change a thing about yourself. There is nothing I want you to do except be your sweet self.

I want you to enjoy this life I've given you and not worry it away. You are special to me and I want you to have it all. I want so badly to give it to you, but you have to let me. You have to listen to me. When I tell you to go somewhere, go. When I give you things to do, then do them. This is my way of helping you. I don't want you to cry and get down. You're too beautiful for that. There is nothing missing, Angie. You are who you are supposed to be.

You can love your family from Colorado. You can enjoy them as if they are right next to you. You can go home whenever you want to. You are never alone. I am always here with you sending you what you need. I will take care of you and protect you for all your days. You will not fail because you are not a failure. You are not unraveling you are becoming. Sometimes we have to come undone before we can be put back together. I'm not trying to make this hard on you, my love. I'm trying to give you time. I will not let you fall. I will provide for you here just as I have every other day of your life.

I wanted better for you. That's true. I wanted more for you than you wanted for yourself and I wanted to show you that you can do anything. Life doesn't feel normal to you right now and it shouldn't. You're not supposed to be okay right now. It's part of your learning and your growth. It's the growth you have wanted whether you can see that right now or not. This is who you have always wanted to be and I'm going to give you what you want. Whether it's hard or not, you deserve to be who you were brought here to be.

I'm proud of you. No matter what I'm proud of you that you are trying. Just don't give up. Please don't give up because I have some really beautiful things here I want to show you that will enrich your life.

Remember you already know what that old life is like now it's time to see another way of life. I never said it would be easy or perfect, but I did say I would walk you through it. This is your path and it may be a little harder than others, but it's because I know you can handle it and you're going to show other people they can handle it too. Just think about all the people you're helping right now whether you think you are or not. This is bigger than you. And you will be rewarded. You just have to be patient and trust.

These struggles are there not to hurt you, but to help you become stronger. You'll get there. I'll get you there just follow me. Even in the darkest moments which you had the other night, you are shedding who you were and that is never easy. But you decided to walk in My light and I will take you places you never thought you could go.

Remember that day on the beach in Cancun when you were at a low. You wanted something more. And I'm giving it to you. You didn't want that life because you knew there was better. Well I haven't forgotten and I'm showing you better. Maybe you feel like you weren't ready for all of this, but you are. You might feel like everything has been taken away from you and it has, but it's so that I can give you all new. You will be happy again. You will. I'm sorry you're going through this but understand it is for your good. You just can't see it yet, but it will come. This too shall pass and be grateful for this time. Whether you realize it or not you're growing closer to me and I want to thank you for following me even in the darkest of times.

When you need to find peace, start looking within. Comfort is fine, but learn how to comfort yourself. What are things you can do? Yoga. Meditation. Prayer. And please don't stop loving yourself. You really are so beautiful and I'm lucky to have you. Don't sit around dwelling in the past, Angie, that is not going to get you anywhere, but back where you don't want to be. And remember you can write to me any time you want.

Angie: Lord, can I ask You anything and You'll always be there to guide me?

God: Yes.

Angie: Lord, will this feeling of homesick leave me?

God: Yes, it will just give it some time.

Angie: Lord, is this really You or am I making this up in my own head?

God: It's really me. This is how I made you. This is one of your spiritual gifts through writing.

Angie: How do I control my emotions?

God: You don't entertain them. You focus on something more productive the moment you notice they are taking hold. You don't allow yourself to think past this moment. The past and the future are places you do not need to go. Just stay here. Don't worry things are going to happen because all you're doing in those moments is attracting that to yourself. You didn't do anything wrong the other day you had to experience that panic so that you'd understand.

Angie: What did I need to learn not to do to myself?

God: Take life so seriously. It's really not serious. Just do the things I put in front of you to do and enjoy what is around you and what I've given you. I don't give everyone the same thing. This is unique for you. This is what you wanted to have and so I'm giving it to you. This is your experience. Don't worry about what others have. You're actually farther along than you realize.

Angie: Do You know how much I love You?

God: Yes, you've shown Me time and time again. The way you talk about Me to others fills My heart with love. I'm so glad you found me. People love your faith. It's so pure and that's new to them. Keep showing people you can do anything so that they know they can do anything. You're showing people it's never too late and share your story. The hard parts of your own story are what's going to help others the most. If they thought it was just easy for you then they wouldn't understand they can do it too. People look at you and think you can do anything, but they don't think the same applies to them so by showing them you're having a hard time they will think they can do it too. It won't be the same things for them as I've given you to do. Their things may be different, but I'm showing them through you doing very big things that they can do the things they would never have done. One day you'll understand why you had to be here. I love you, Angie, keep going, sweet girl.

Angie: Lord, will I feel that freshness and newness here, that freedom that I've been waiting for?

God: Yes, you will. You definitely will. It's just going to take a little time for you to feel it, but you will. You see you're still working through some old stuff. Things don't magically click overnight and you still had some stuff you're holding onto.

For some reason, you thought you were going to come here and be a new person. The thing is you don't need to be a new person, you are who you are and you'll never be anyone different and I don't want you to be. Starting new has nothing to do with not having your old connections. You should still have those old connections. That's your foundation and your support so use those networks and people especially as you're going through this transition. That will help you feel like yourself, but also make room for new people and new connections to enter. I will continue to send people to you who are good for you here. They won't be any better or any worse than people back home and you needed to learn this. People are people anywhere you go it's just their outlook that may be different.

I know this was a painful lesson you just learned arriving here, but it's one that you needed to understand. There are not better people or worse people. And this doesn't mean you should go back home it's just helping you to become more humble. And it's ok when some relationships tend to not be as strong anymore, but the thing is you really love people and that's one of your greatest gifts. It's not hard for you to relate and care about others because to you people are the most important thing in the world. Do you see how far along you are with that? Not everyone gets that, Angie. You get it and you feel it. It's like ripping off a band aid just for you to come here alone. But I want to show you that you can still have those relationships without having to live in their circumstances.

You have your own set of circumstances and you've made good choices for your life. You've lived at a higher level than some to set a good example of how you can choose to live and choose to treat others. Don't you see that now? And this has been a good lesson for you in trusting others and letting them support you. You needed a lot of support this week and you went after it instead of being all alone in your suffering. This is something you wouldn't have done before and look, you reached out to so many people and in doing that they were there to help you make a decision that was hard for you to make on your own. By sharing what you're going through others are able to share what they went through with similar situations because you are not the first to go through something like this. It may be unique to you in how you are responding or that you don't have anyone out here with you, but I did that because I knew you didn't need it. You're different than a lot of people whether you want to believe it or not. I've tried showing you this your whole life, but you haven't accepted it yet. You will. Right now you're still comparing yourself to everyone else. I have set you apart. You have something very unique to accomplish here. It doesn't have to feel like a burden. Let it feel more like a gift.

Angie: So I want to write about forgiveness and letting go. Will You walk me through this process? What does it mean?

God: It means that you replace the hatred with love. This is the only way you can truly forgive. You reframe your thoughts about the person or situation you're forgiving. Instead of thinking this person wronged you and holding onto the anger and pain you reframe it. You think about the person in the best possible light you can. When a memory pops up with them in it, you see the beauty that came from it. When you can see in a beautiful way what the experience or person brought to your journey you can appreciate it. This doesn't mean you have to dwell on it. You just simply shift when you catch yourself slipping into that old pattern or blaming or feeling the hurt that was caused. You learn to accept it for what it was. The love you send the other person's way releases the pain from affecting your life today. It keeps you at an elevated level where you can appreciate the life you are living today. When you don't forgive you are literally living in the past and that's a painful place to dwell because you have no control over it and can't move forward.

A few weeks after I stumbled upon writing to God, as if by divine intervention, I found myself in a bookstore on Pearl Street in downtown Boulder in the metaphysical section, which I always seem to be drawn to. A book on the lower shelf screamed out to me, as I opened the cover the answer to my question from a few days earlier about my being able to talk to God presented itself. I had found a book replicating exactly what I had encountered. The book *Conversations with God* by Neale Donald Walsh had found its way to me to validate my encounter with speaking to God. As I opened up the book it was all about conversations Neale had with God and God giving him wisdom and guidance. The answer to why I had come to Colorado was just found. We can choose to shrug these encounters off as coincidence or we can embrace them for what they are, signs that are Heaven sent to show us we are not out of our mind, but instead getting closer to our spiritual gifts and abilities. These validations we come across are there as little winks to tell us we are on path and what we found is indeed true for us. I've continued my chats with God and each time I have them, I'm filled with a peace and love that comes from no one other than the One who made me.

Some of us have been chosen to be teachers. Let me dig into my thought a little more. I want to preface this part of the book with this thought, we are all teachers and we are all learners simultaneously. Throughout our lives, the teachings and the learnings may look different as we naturally change, evolve and grow. What I challenge you with is to find out what your teaching is supposed to be. For me one of my teachings and probably equally my lesson is to live in a way that is truly authentic to me. To not buy into all the rules society wants to force upon our lives. When one person, in one city, can show up as themselves with no reservations they inadvertently teach those around them that it's okay to be themselves too. Part of my teaching that it's okay to be yourself is sharing the pieces of myself that I have stumbled upon. My chat with God is as an example that we all have our own gifts and God wants us to share them. I knew just as soon as I wrote my talk with God that He wanted me to add it to my book whether I was comfortable with it or not. It is truly one of the most vulnerable parts of my story to tell. When I think of all the people it could help, I have no choice but to share it. It's me being who I really am. When we do this, it is a gift and a treasure among treasures.

There were other gifts I stumbled upon during my time in Colorado. One of them came in the form of a woman whose name I would learn was, Maria Dancing Heart Hoagland, and I would soon consider her to be a kindred spirit. Being new to Colorado, God answered my prayer for a new friend, by putting Maria on my path. The first moment I met, Maria, as she sat down next to me at a networking event to share her healing and bereavement work, I knew she was going to play a special role in my life and I just had to know her. I was drawn to her wonderfully unique, gentle and loving soul. She quickly showed me what it looks like to live in God's purpose. The truth is, Maria, helped me during a tough transition in my life to see the deeper meaning to our experiences. It always felt like she had secrets about living and dying that only God chose to share with her. Which made sense given her life's work and the wisdom that just oozed out of her very being.

Maria and I delighted in taking sun filled walks together and making a cup of hot tea afterwards. Our encounter was one of divinity. Our Sunday walk-and-talks covered a lot of ground as we would discuss how amazing it was to find someone who shared a similar passion for helping others heal through the experience of grief, longing for love in our lives, and all our hopes and dreams to do the work we were brought here to do. Most importantly our talks about our deep commitment to our faith and spirituality made me feel at home. It felt like we were old friends, as if our souls had known one another for centuries.

Needless to say, Maria had a profound impact on my life even if our time together on this Earth was only for a brief moment. This is the interesting thing about meeting others from our soul tribe, they show up in our lives exactly at the right moment. She, too, was called to support others through grief and may have been one of the first people to share so passionately my desire to help people look at death and the dying process in a different light bringing the spiritual realm to these topics in such a way that we could hopefully gain some momentum on accepting death in this country. There is so much suffering when it comes to grief and to find someone else who longed to alleviate some of the misconceptions of dying and the afterlife was no short of a miracle. Maria had already published several books herself on the topic, which gave me great motivation to finish mine.

We would talk about how lucky we both felt to have found someone in this barren time in both of our lives to fill some of the empty space with light, understanding, warmth, and love. You see the truth is we never really know when it's our turn to go, but I wholeheartedly believe we each signed up to cross paths with certain souls, a reunion if you will from home, from the other side, from which we came. Making my Colorado time written in the stars long before I even identified with journeying there. In the bigger picture of my life, my soul had something to see there, certain souls to meet, something to learn and lots to experience. Whether my head will ever understand it all I'll never know, but my heart found some true gems there. And my dear friend Maria was one of them. Maria felt more like a teacher to me than most.

Our paths didn't stay connected for nearly as long as I would have liked. I hadn't known then what the short outcome of our reunion would be, only that she touched my life and changed a bit of me like the great ones do. I would find out a little over a year after seeing Maria for the last time that her time on Earth had come to an end. My first thought when hearing the sad news was how Maria was a true teacher until the very end. I'm positive her death took her home soaring on wings of an Angel, high above the daily chatter of human life, to find her peaceful resting place among the clouds, at one with our Creator honoring a life well lived, one in service to doing her work. Now that's an example all of us can learn from.

Every so often I park myself in a seat in front of my computer to spend some time listening to Maria's teachings. What I find most inspiring about her is her absolute resolve and confidence in who God sent her here to be. She's herself, no questions asked, she is a spiritual being living her life in reverence to her gifts, not being afraid of them, but instead using them to help others. Not allowing herself to be dimmed by the darkness, but illuminated by the light. We should all work towards that level of commitment to our divine plan.

I include Maria in my Colorado chapter because she was my Colorado chapter. During a time of what felt like great loss knowing her was a great win on my part and one I'll always be thankful for our time together. Yes, we all go through trying times and it's our choice to either take the gifts and remember the lessons or toss it all out as a bad experience. I'll choose to take the lessons, but also take the love I found in new relationships. Ones I never would have had if the experience hadn't presented itself and I hadn't taken it. Because really, isn't that what it's all about anyways?

We can't stop change from happening. We have to grow and evolve and with that comes change. But the love, my friends, the love always remains, that is in fact the only thing that is truly eternal and unending. I can still feel Maria's presence when I'm calm and still. I know she's there rooting me on to continue "our work" the work that God gave us to share. When I think about her, I imagine her passing the baton on to me and me taking it reluctantly knowing I have big shoes to fill and that I want to make her proud. See we're never alone even when we don't understand why seemingly "bad" things happen. Now when someone I know and love passes I can feel a sense of joy for them knowing they fulfilled their time here on Earth and God called them home. Where they are is so much better than anything we can ever imagine or experience on this planet.

God wants us to find joy and belonging and purpose here in the hopes that one day we will be able to better align our energies with where we come from in Heaven. God truly does want us to find peace on Earth, but He can't come down and do our work for us. We all have a calling, we all have a purpose. Many purposes throughout the span of our lives, but we must be the ones to fulfill our purpose, no one can do it for us. To know what your calling is, is a gift and a burden simultaneously. If you are eager enough to find out what your calling is chances are you would like to live it, manifest it and experience it. The first takes some insight, the second takes some guts. You have both and I know without a doubt if God reveals your calling, He has a way for you to fulfill it. Fulfillment first starts with mastering trust. The old saying, "trust is a must", is much truer than we give it credit for. You will see your life begin to change when you trust that it will. You don't get to see it and then believe it. You must first believe it before you will see it.

You only get to the peak by going through the valley.

My Colorado chapter is still a blur to me. There are days where I look back on my time there fondly and then there are moments that I can still feel the knot of despair in the pit of my stomach, the ache and longing for peace. Our days are marked by moments that change our lives forever. Colorado taught me if you really want to do something you must do it with blind faith that you will get the lessons and the outcomes out of it that are meant just for you. We may not always like the outcome, but there is always something worth exploring. I felt like "failure" defined that period in my life, a daunting load I carried within myself feeling like I had just lost everything. There was nothing standing on the other side of my faith to catch me when my sails went limp and my wings forgot how to open so I could fly. There was only one way back down to Earth and it felt like me hitting the ground with a big thump. The same ground that I so firmly stood on before embarking on my biggest journey of faith thus far.

I remember people telling me how brave I was to go off on my own, to have such faith that it would all work out, leaving everyone I'd known and loved behind to explore another way of being. What I wouldn't realize for a few more months was that my Colorado chapter did just that, it gave me clarity, where I didn't have it before. I slowly started realizing I didn't want to be anywhere else but home with my family in Nebraska. I now had the clarity I had been searching for all along. The move back home would be different than the move to Colorado. I was going back home knowing it was where I had to be to be happy, not just someplace I ended up.

Making the decision for myself that this is the life I wanted in Nebraska, with the people I wanted to share my life with, made the restlessness in my soul before the move cease to exist. I had ups and downs during those months in Colorado, more than I feel comfortable admitting. Never had I known how difficult and downright depressing recreating your life could be. Everything was new for me. There wasn't a single street that looked familiar. Some days I didn't speak to a single soul unless it was my mom calling to check on me. Other days I went out about town attending Meetup groups to connect with other entrepreneurs who felt a similar call as I did to do something meaningful with their lives, on their own terms, in their own way. Other days I couldn't drag myself out of bed because I simply didn't know what to do with myself that day. There was no work to be done, no family or friends to meet up with and no real reason to not just hang out by myself all day. On those days. I prayed. I prayed a lot. I felt so purposeful before the move, so resilient, so alive. And now all I felt was a big heap of regret, tossed in the middle of some self-loathing, dished up on a plate of "what in the world just happened to my life?"

Feeling lost wasn't always so bad when I had the mountains to take my mind off it. There were times all I needed was some fresh mountain air to remind myself why I chose to come to Colorado in the first place. The scenery was hard to replicate anywhere else with its white snow caps and winding mountain roads taking me one step closer to Heaven. The friendships I made along the way are some that I will never forget and I will always cherish. It turned out there was a lot of good that came from this time in my life, once again showing me that with each new adventure comes with it lessons that we may never want to learn, but ones that are necessary. As I look back at that time in my life I'm so grateful that I took the plunge. Had I not taken that chance I'd still be sitting here wishing I could be brave enough to take that leap of faith to move to Colorado, but instead I'm sitting here sufficiently at peace that I did, and that it led me home to myself, to accepting who I really am, a born and raised Nebraska girl.

Chapter Nine

Faith Walk

"It is in the act of offering our hearts in faith that something in us transforms...proclaiming that we no longer stand on the sidelines but are leaping directly into the center of our lives, our truth, our full potential."
-Sharon Salzberg

What does it really mean to live with or without faith? I'm guessing just like me you've heard the phrase "keep the faith" before. Maybe you've heard it during a challenging time in your life. I never really understood what it meant until all I had was my faith. It's during the valleys that seep into our very existence that it's most difficult to embody those three words to really "keep the faith." Those times when nothing seems to be working out the way we expected even when we tried our very best and still our expectations aren't being met. Expectations and faith don't go hand in hand.

After a particularly rough go of it in Colorado, after really putting my life on the line to chase my dreams and ending up back at the drawing board, is when I needed faith the most. I realized I needed time to heal after trying to figure it all out on my own and still not getting much further than where I was before taking my "faith walk" into the unknown. Even after listening to my inner guidance and believing so much in the law of attraction I felt more lost than found.

A few months after returning home to Omaha, I found myself at a yoga class during savasana asking God to speak to me. I hadn't been able to hear Him much lately, probably because of all the needless worry that was filling my mind. For a brief moment, as I lay on my back, eyes closed, in total surrender, I heard His words again. Words I desperately needed to hear. The thing about God is, He shows up when we are silent. And the words He spoke still resonate to this very day. He said, "Angie, faith is believing even when there is no evidence." A tear slid down my cheek. In my heart, I knew what He was trying to tell me. That no matter how things looked and felt right now, my faith is what would get me where I wanted to go, living the life I knew I was created to live. Without my faith, I knew I would give up. It all felt too hard and confusing.

You see I've known for quite some time that God is calling me towards doing the work I was meant for with writing, life coaching, spiritual teaching, healing work, and speaking. Laying on that dimly lit yoga studio floor I still felt far from living the life I'd dreamed of and envisioned. The faith in which God talked to me about that evening showed me that I could still get there. If I truly wanted to teach about faith I had to become intimate with it. I had no evidence surrounding me that little by little my world would begin to shift into my truest purpose, my most authentic life. God was teaching me a big lesson on that floor. He was building my faith. He was taking me from being a believer when I see the evidence to a believer without having to see the evidence. He was taking me from needing evidence to having faith, to understanding I've had faith all along. I walked the path even with nothing in my reality showing me it was going to happen. I already did believe. I already had faith. And now I understood the difference. We can always choose to live in faith. Faith that even when things don't look like they are turning out, they really are. We don't have to have our dream in the palm of our hand, living it, for our dream to be valid and real. It's inside us even when we don't see it on the outside.

Faith and belief go hand in hand. We must have faith and believe we can achieve the things that seem far beyond our control. I found that I was focusing on the things I felt I could control because those were somehow within my power until I realized nothing is really in my control at all. God is the giver of life and with His support I can achieve anything. The only thing holding us back from having what we want is our beliefs around whether it's possible. When we recognize we don't have faith or need to change a belief we need to first go to God and ask for Him to help us to have faith and to believe. We don't get it from anywhere else outside of God. This has been the single greatest gift I have been given, the realization that all my needs are taken care of through God. When I'm weary and feel like my hope is slipping all I need to do is ask Him for more hope and He always provides.

They say everything happens for a reason. We must trust the reason will make itself known in time. And until then believe there's a reason for everything. There's life happening behind the scenes, things only God knows. But He also knows how to grab our attention, to wake us up and that's reason enough. Anxiety is caused by wanting to be someplace other than where we are right now. Learning to trust that we are where we're meant to be at all times helps relieve an anxious state of being. We are each capable of creating the life we want – it is possible! Playing a victim to our lives only leaves us feeling disempowered with an overall sense of being defeated. This is all an illusion. The mind willingly travels down whatever road you would like to take it on. It's a willing partner. Master your mind and master your life. Put more good thoughts in than you take out and you will soon notice a shift. Listen to that voice within to help guide and shape your decisions. I'm challenging putting labels on things that don't work out the way we anticipated as "failure." We throw this term around very loosely in our society. When something doesn't "work out" we associate it with having failed. This doesn't sit right in my gut. Every time I hear someone say, "we must fail before we succeed", or "don't feel like you failed", or "you'll eventually learn something from your failure", I want to scream, "No!" We must stop doing this to ourselves and others. True failure is not trying to go after something you really want in life. Sitting back and letting life pass you by is the real harm not going for it. Going for it is never failure. You see, dear ones, the essence of living is in the pursuit, in the trying. When we try, that is success. But when we really go for it, wow, that's living. There is nothing close to failure in giving it your all, exploring, experiencing.

We base so much of our thoughts on success in monetary terms. If things aren't going well financially there must not be success. We have it all wrong. Sometimes success is in the waking up in the morning to go at it again. We need to learn to be less harsh with ourselves and with the world around us. Our expectations can be so high that we set impossible goals for ourselves. When we don't live up to them we punish ourselves, or worse yet those around us, with our unmet expectations that turned into resentment somewhere along the way, because we were too hard on ourselves when things didn't go exactly as planned. As if we were ever one hundred percent in control of the outcomes in the first place. We are powerful beyond measure and there are times we also need to be reminded that we don't have the ability to control everything and we shouldn't want to. We do our best and yet we don't always believe our best is good enough.

If you have tried at something, I mean really tried, heart, soul, time invested then you have succeeded. End of story. You are a success. When we flip our terms of success and acknowledge all the successes and steps we have already made we can declare to ourselves that we are not giving up. Giving up is meant for the meek and mild and you're neither. If you have stepped outside of your comfort zone to find a different way there is nothing meek about you. This is where being stubborn pays off. Dig your heels in, fight the good fight, keep at your goals no matter how many steps you still need to take. Do it from a place of heart centered awareness and have faith things will turn out just as they are meant to. Understanding in all humility that you will get where you want to be when the time is right. Perhaps you still have lessons to learn, but you will get there.

When we are able to look at life as the teacher and us as the student we can glean lessons, wisdom and unconventional knowledge. When we master this skill, we are able to get something out of everything we go through even in the darkest times of despair. If you are from the mindset that life is only good and valuable when it feels good to you, you will miss out on a whole lot of hard, but valuable lessons. Your mindset about what is valuable in life needs to shift. Think of it like this, in partnership with God my soul decided it was time to come to Earth to learn more valuable lessons, to experience joy and pain, not just one or the other. I rather like this soul that I'm entrusted with carrying around and I rather appreciate this body that allows me to do it. To have appreciation for the light and the dark within each one of our journeys is to allow life to be what it is meant to be instead of trying to fight the dark feelings that tend to creep in during the rough patches of life. If our mindset is that life is meant to be free of pain, sorrow, anxiety, worry and any other emotion that we consider "negative" then we wouldn't see how the human spirit can persevere through these lows to re-engage with the highs of life. Our society becomes addicted to feeling good and doing anything in our power to flee the negative emotions when they pop up. People consume alcohol, take drugs, become addicted to collecting more and more stuff all in the name of not feeling life. We need more stillness, more compassion and more understanding to combat some of these addictive behaviors that can steal the very experience of aliveness. Instead of numbing ourselves we should sit with ourselves especially in the shadows.

These emotions that bubble up to the surface are trying to scream out to us, to pay attention to what we are trying so desperately to escape. There is something bigger at play here. We each have supports on the other side who are helping to guide and align our path even during those times when we believe we are off course they are always there to help guide us back. Our emotions can be so painful and overwhelming during times of loss, change, or transition that we may think we will never feel normal again. This isn't true. You'll feel passion again, you'll get your energy and stamina back. You won't be depressed forever. You'll rise and when you do, oh when you do it will be a day worth celebrating. It's a process. It takes time to bounce back after a fall. Take your time, be patient and kind with yourself when you're recovering from a trauma. This is what I had to learn after moving back home from Colorado and boy am I glad I did. I came across so many healing modalities that I never would have known were possible if I hadn't experienced the need to be healed. It brought me to find more pieces of myself once again. Leading me down a path I am so grateful I took. One that had Colorado not have happened I most likely would never have stumbled upon. I sit here today as a Reiki Master because I needed healing. The healing and intuitive guidance sessions I do with clients is what God was preparing me for all of this time. I understand my clients because of what I have been through.

The person with faith will succeed in the end. When we can't see something it's easy to get discouraged, but to fully acquire the biggest potential for our lives we must believe even when there is no evidence and everything in our reality points to the contrary. That's what faith is all about. Keep going back to what you know to be true in your heart and every little thing will be okay. We also must learn to be realistic and patient with our endeavors. None of us got to where we are today overnight and we won't get where we are going overnight either. It would be too overwhelming for us to make major life changes in the matter of mere days or even months. When we are thrust into new situations without being ready it can take a toll on us so take time to get where you're going. You don't have to figure it all out today or tomorrow. Keep walking in faith towards the goals you set for your life and you'll get there in due time.

Chapter Ten

A Time to Heal

*"There is a time for everything,
and a season for every activity under the heavens:
a time to be born and a time to die,
a time to plant and a time to uproot,
a time to kill and a time to heal,
a time to tear down and a time to build,
a time to weep and a time to laugh,
a time to mourn and a time to dance,
a time to scatter stones and a time to gather them,
a time to embrace and a time to refrain from embracing,
a time to search and a time to give up,
A time to keep and a time to throw away,
A time to tear and a time to mend,
A time to be silent and a time to speak,
A time to love and a time to hate,
A time for war and a time for peace."*
Ecclesiastes 3:1-8

There will come a day when each one of us is faced with our own worst nightmare. It's going to happen. The old saying, "it's not a matter of if, it's a matter of when", is the reality of our lives. I don't say this to worry or upset you. I say it to show you that everyone goes through it. To show you that you are not alone. You are living similar experiences as everyone else. We are more alike than we are different. We all want to do something meaningful with our lives, we are all searching for that thing we can put our mark on in the world and it's out there for all of us. Some of us will pursue that mark and some will only dream of it, but we are all capable of it. It's not a matter of "can" it's a matter of "will." Good old will power. Will you rise to stand in your own authentic power to become the person you long to be? Or will you take the easy way out?

The easy way is an option, too. You can choose that path, or you can choose the more difficult, longer, sometimes down right tumultuous road that lay ahead of you to get to that place you know somewhere deep inside that awaits you. I've taken the hard road. To be honest I'm not sure why. The hard road hasn't always led me where I wanted to go or been my friend. It's been the exact opposite at times. But I've still taken it. Not because I wasn't afraid or worried about where it was going to lead me, but because it's the one that made me feel the most alive. The most purposeful and the most guided. I was led to this road and there were times I questioned and doubted why this road was the road my Maker chose for me. There were times I was downright angry with God for leading me to a place I didn't feel I could be happy in let alone handle. It's easy to look back and try to find the gems or nuggets of truth in those roads, but when you remember the pain they caused you, you know it wasn't as easy as it looked.

Take my road to Colorado for example. That was going to be my new beginning, so I thought. It did end up with me accepting myself for who I really am, who I always was, and who I will always be. I didn't find someone new once I crossed the state line, I only found more of myself. I found the part of myself that was ready to give the real me a helping hand, lifting her up, dusting her off to give her exactly what she had been looking for all of these years. My love and my total acceptance. The person I always dreamed I would be didn't look so appealing any more once I finally realized I liked who I already was. She was hopeful despite pain, she was aware despite the confusion and at the root of who she was, was grace, always longing to do something great with her life to help and uplift others. I finally realized circumstances no longer mattered, I could be anywhere as long as I was right with myself on the inside. In the searching

I found that I was already who I wanted to be. It's funny how life works out. We must wander away from something to see it for what it truly is. If we think we are the sole creator of our own lives we are making a big assumption that just isn't true. We are a co-creator with God. That is such a comforting realization.

The things I've had happen in my life have taught me there is a middle road. One I haven't always walked down as I've somewhat preferred living on the edges. The edges of joy, by really going after life, or the edges of sorrow, where I feel there is so much to learn. I've never really liked that middle road where things are just sort of unfolding naturally in their own time. This road is the most boring road for me, yet there is an equal amount of living and learning that the middle road gives as a gift to those who are patient enough to understand what this road is all about. This road isn't for the ones who want to grasp at life until the last drop, ending up stalling out before the end, and it's not for those who want to wallow in the depths of despair where you feel every bit of life from that sacred space. The space where we feel alive in our suffering. No, the middle space is neither of these. The middle space is where peace lives. Where we have a firm understanding of what life is and isn't. The middle space is kinder on our souls. It allows us to take our time to learn our lessons and not have to cram it all in, in one sitting. Sometimes we need this middle space, as if a pause button has been placed on our lives from God to ensure we have gathered up every last morsel of learning in the way only a pause can teach us. This time helps prepare us for the propelled launch He has in store for us. We must grow our wings before we are able to take flight. God can either step in and perform a miracle or allow us to grow out of the lack of forward momentum. This allows us to shed the weight our past has put on us so that once the pause button is lifted we emerge as lighter beings truer to the essence and nature which we are made of.

If He is indeed the potter and we are the clay there will ultimately be times in our lives, for each of us, where the potter must allow the clay to morph, mold and move into new shapes. Perhaps turning into shapes the potter never even imagined.

Doesn't this just excite you? We have the ability to show God what we are made of. We can take the bare bones of who He alone made us to be and become something even more spectacular than He envisioned. With a little gentle pressure from the potter we can transform into something even grander than our hearts have imagined. When you are in a place of pause, where nothing seems like it's working out in your favor, the light is still up ahead in the distance and you remain in the darkness searching for any tiny bit of hope, always remember you are being reborn into something even more beautiful than you could ever have imagined. Rebirth is not easy. There is a lot of pushing and pulling, letting go, giving in, and an extreme amount of faith that it takes to truly believe somewhere in your shattered heart that you are that phoenix who will rise from the ashes. Stronger, more resilient, braver, and more beautiful for having allowed this great big Universe to reshape who you are from the inside out so that you can do the work you were designed to do in this world. For many of us, it doesn't happen overnight. We would like it to be as easy as flipping on the microwave for three minutes and boom we're done and ready to go on to new things, but the letting go and becoming process often takes longer than we would like.

There are those in life that try to skate by without enduring a tragedy or hardship and then there are those of us who lean into them to try to understand them instead of avoiding the fallout from them. There are certain days that we never want to come, they are usually days that bring an ending. Endings are rough as they seem to force us to have to live a different way. To embrace fresh new beginnings, we must allow endings to come into our lives. Please be patient, and better yet kind to yourself for you will get where you're going, it may just not be in your timing. You don't have to overhaul your life overnight, you are more than welcome to do it piece by piece, step by step so you can enjoy the journey. The difference here is that our circumstances may change so our lives may look outwardly different, we can grow spiritually, we can push ourselves to take better care of ourselves, but the core of who we are is innately perfect and good. That's the way we were created to be and nothing can take that from us.

All our emotions are sacred not just the ones that feel good. The ones that feel hard are just as sacred as all the rest. These are the ones we must use to transform and ultimately show us where we need healing the most. Feeling healed is the best feeling in the world. Feeling as though you need healed is one of the worst. The kind of feeling that gnaws at you, keeping you tethered, looking outside of yourself for your own sense of peace. We are far more powerful than we let on and when it comes to healing it's no different. We intuitively know what we need to let go of, and what we need to do to heal ourselves. It might just be time. Time is the greatest healer at our disposal. Give yourself time. Time can be all we need to shift our perspective on something that once felt painful. Time might just end up telling you a different story. When we long for healing it could be there is a wound we keep picking at.

Healing comes in many forms. One of those is acceptance. When we can accept things as they are we free ourselves up to begin anew. What I've come to understand is, we don't always get the answers we are asking for in life. We can try to understand why certain things happen, but we don't always even get to understanding. That's why I'm a fan of lessons learned. Lessons learned presumes we don't have all the answers to the questions that plague us. Instead we can have peace in the unanswered questions in life. Getting out of situations the gems of learning that came from it and then promptly moving on without forgetting the lesson is a good way to move forward. Remembering you came here for the experience and to leave your mark on life, hopefully leaving it a better place than when you arrived. You're not here to carry around a big old suitcase that is labeled "here is my baggage, all my mistakes, shame and guilt." Instead carry the lessons with you and leave the rest. We can choose to either let our experiences define us or refine us. Being defined by our experiences and allowing them to shape who we are is a less empowering approach to life. Allowing our experiences to refine who we are and making us a better person for having lived it is more empowering. It's always a choice.

I believe our life depends upon how we choose to handle the struggles and obstacles in life that really shape who we are as a person. It's always been a comfort to me to acknowledge that every single experience we have has the potential for healing, in its own time and in its own way. There is no healing without forgiveness. They go hand in hand. At the base of most of our struggles is the inability to forgive something or someone from our past. When we go through the many layers of forgiveness we arrive at healing. It's like the peeling of an onion we must first start with the outside layer to go within. Forgiveness is not always a one-time process. We must forgive little by little. Day by day. Step by step. It takes energy to forgive and it's a spiritual process. To forgive someone else or ourselves is to admit imperfection. The freedom that comes with forgiveness is exponential. When we choose to forgive we choose to see the humanity in another and within ourselves. It's letting someone off the hook for doing something you wished they hadn't and it's allowing ourselves to be less than perfect, giving grace to our shadows. Releasing our guilt.

Guilt. This word alone makes us feel guilt. When we hold onto what we think we should have done we are living in the past, feeling guilty for something that we can't change. This is never a good way to feel or to be, but we are only human and we are brought here with so many experiences that add up that there is no wonder why we feel guilty for the way we have treated people or things we wish we could change.

Let's take a look at where these feelings of guilt come from. Often we don't recognize we are holding onto guilt from as far back as our childhood. We can conjure up feelings of guilt when we didn't treat someone the way we wish we would have, or when we treated a loved one in a less than desirable way. Where there is guilt, we are holding onto shame for an action we did that wasn't out of the loving part of our natures. There is only one thing we can do to release this guilt. Forgive it and let it go. Many of us hold onto guilt because we don't know how to let it go. We are so conditioned to feel badly about past mistakes, decisions and feel so much pressure to be perfect that we are afraid of who we will be without our same old stories. The truth is forgiving and letting go of our past is the most brave and courageous thing we can do in our lives.

Forgiveness is a loving act of kindness that only we can give ourselves. No one can do it for us and we don't need someone else to say they forgive us to be willing to forgive ourselves. If you have someone to forgive that is coming to your mind as you read this remember people treat you how they feel about themselves, the hurtful things that happen to us in life are never about us. They are about the other person, but our limited understanding makes it feel like it's about us, and holds us back from this understanding. If someone is acting out towards you they are typically projecting the way they feel about themselves onto you.

To forgive another is to set yourself free. Freedom from the unneeded bondage we tether ourselves to. When we set out on the path towards forgiveness we commit to more freedom in our lives. Part of the reason forgiveness is difficult is it empties us of holding on to our same old stories. Without them we must re-identify ourselves with something new and different and leave the old and worn out behind. By forgiving our past it opens space for us to be something new and different in the present.

We aren't always comfortable being someone we don't know yet. The reality is we run away from our freedom too often because we are more comfortable living in the patterns of our lives instead of reinventing something new and different. The thing about forgiveness is that it brings change with it and it has the ability to uproot all we've ever known. The tried and true, although not always exciting, presents us with stability, which in itself is a good thing. However, when we cling to it and give it more value than it deserves it can hold us back from really going for the things we want in life. I'm not suggesting we should give up a perfectly happy life to chase some wild fantasy, I'm suggesting we be brave enough with our lives that we do something meaningful with them.

I feel like there's an epidemic happening in our country where so many of us are choosing the safe path, the path with least resistance that we aren't stretching ourselves in the directions we really want to go in our hearts. I am all for taking care of ourselves and having the means to do so does call for the need to be responsible. But I don't think it means abandoning the desires of our hearts. We can tend towards one extreme or the other. I've been there myself. We either risk it all to follow our inner voice or we don't even allow ourselves the pleasure of picking up a paintbrush, taking voice lessons or getting involved in community theater. Both extremes lead to either overwhelm with jumping all in or underwhelm our lives to the point where we are lethargic before our feet even hit the floor in the morning. Both lead to depression, anxiety and eventual exhaustion. To heal we must allow ourselves to chase our dreams.

What I'm suggesting is that the middle ground is a great place where small, but mighty steps may be taken in the direction of our dreams. I've done it both ways. And I'd say that the balance of having it all is the sweetest spot we can find. The one where we know we can put food on the table, pay our bills, and still work towards our most delicious life. The one where we take intentional steps in the right direction. If you have given up on that big dream of yours I beg you to reconsider. We all get down on ourselves, may feel like giving up, but God wants us to realize our fullest potential, our greatest life, our most prized way of spending our time. There's wisdom that comes in trying, there's even more wisdom in not giving up. The winds of life will come knocking, let them in. All of them. Especially the ones you are most afraid of, the ones where you'll be suspended in mid-air not knowing what direction to turn. This is when the sweet whispers of your own soul will trudge forward, a safe distance between you and what's out there calling your name. The soul always knows more than the mind. Let it be your guide, like a beacon in the night calling you home to yourself.

There are times I wonder if guilt is just a manmade emotion to keep people living in fear. Since God is not of fear and instead of love, guilt cannot possibly be an emotion created of His will. However, we can't rush the forgiveness process. And we can't forgive before we're ready to. The beauty is you can forgive whenever you decide to forgive. It doesn't have to take a lifetime to forgive all it takes is a decision to do it. We embody a much larger capacity to forgive than we let on. Forgiveness was never really about the other person it was always about you. Not forgiving is making the decision that it is more important to hold onto the grudge than be released from it. Sometimes we hold on out of fear. Fear of not knowing who we are without holding on to the moments we feel define our existence. If we let go of the anger, hurt, and resentment people or experiences caused us what are we left with? If we escape the pain of the past it opens our present to have a different outcome and that's not always easy to take on and embrace. Who are we without the hurt someone else caused? Not forgiving keeps us small and only requires us to survive the hurt that was caused. Forgiveness on the other hand requires us to expand our current way of thinking. Not forgiving allows us to keep up with our same old stories from the past. Forgiving requires us to let go of the excuses we've used perhaps our entire lives. We get so comfortable playing our "assigned" roles that we can easily ride these out our entire lives. Wouldn't it be a shame at the end of the line to look back and see that we could have chosen to forgive but instead we chose to be bitter. The point here is that not forgiving hurts you and forgiving helps you. It's your choice.

Many of us think that to forgive someone means that we are okay with the action we feel has wrongly been made against us. In reality it means that we are no longer interested in carrying around the pain associated with it. We are ready and, more often than not, we are simply willing to let go of the stories we continue to relive. Not forgiving is powerlessness, as if someone has held something over us. Being the forgiver is powerful. At the root of forgiveness is our belief that we ourselves are worthy of forgiveness. Have you ever done something you regret? Maybe treated a stranger or loved one less than what your heart truly desired? If the answer is yes, welcome to being human. The majority of the time when we feel resistance to forgiving it's because deep down we don't feel worthy of forgiveness ourselves or perhaps we want to hold onto the anger.

Take a minute to really consider this, does it resonate? I am less likely to have the capacity to forgive someone else when I don't believe I deserve to be forgiven. When we constantly hold ourselves to standards that only God could possess we in turn hold others to those same standards whether we consciously realize this or not. There is not always a rational explanation for how we feel, but when those feelings of shame, guilt, or not being enough surface, they are a good indicator that we may be putting those same feelings of unworthiness onto those around us. Subconsciously, thinking we're not worthy of forgiveness so the other person surely isn't either. Thus, the cycle continues.

Now here's what I want you to really let sink in and remember. You are worthy of forgiveness and forgiving. They both affect you, not anyone else. Your ability to forgive yourself is critical here. It's an internal job. You can't begin to learn how to forgive another until you do the work on forgiving yourself. I can think of numerous times where I reacted in a way that made me feel bad about myself and I beat myself up for it day after day. The smaller things in life like getting upset with other drivers, or not being as polite as I could be to a cashier because I clearly was not having the best day. The bigger things in life like feeling guilty for years that my marriage didn't work out or not doing more for those I love or even snapping at those closest to me. If we can't get to the place where we can say to ourselves that we're human and not made to be perfect, but that we are all perfectly imperfect then we will never allow others to be human and make mistakes if we can't allow ourselves to make them. Part of the guilt and un-forgiveness we carry in ourselves stems from not knowing how to correct the offense and instead we just carry it with us without releasing it.

Take the example of snapping at a cashier. Instead of recognizing our snappiness in the moment and correcting the behavior in real time more often than not we carry our grouchy mood throughout the interaction, get in the car and then the guilt sinks in. We aren't proud of who we were in the interaction with the cashier and we let it affect us the rest of the day. It's in the moment of recognition where we can make the most difference to release our guilt and turn our mood around. What I'm suggesting we should do more is correct the behaviors that caused us the guilt in the first place. Again, taking the example of the cashier, if in the interaction we have a moment of clarity to witness ourselves not being our best self we are able to switch sooner. In the moment, we can then turn it around and say to the cashier while we are still standing in front of them that we're sorry and that we just caught ourselves being a little abrasive or unkind. Catching our actions in the moment helps us to release our guilt by apologizing and fixing the situation. Instead we tend to not confess our misdoings and carry the guilt inside which only stacks on top of more guilt.

When we hold onto things from the past it only holds us back from what we truly want to experience in life. We talk about forgiveness often and we truly want to be able to forgive others in an effort to be free from the burdens we carry. On some basic level, we all understand that when we don't forgive it only harms our being. It's the worst feeling to experience, not forgiving is what keeps us stuck in the past and unable to move forward with our lives. I believe we want to truly live for today, but somehow we get stuck in looking back. For many of us we want new ways of being and new patterns to develop to be more successful in all areas of our lives to include our relationships, our outlook on life, our careers, our finances and to see that we can live a life of our choosing. By not forgiving ourselves and others of the past we end up drawing the same types of experiences into our current reality.

For example, if you haven't been able to forgive yourself for overspending on a credit card you carry that guilty with you from the past experience and recreate it in the future. However, if you are able to forgive how you managed your finances in the past you would be freed up to no longer need to repeat the past behaviors that got you there in the first place. Until you make amends with how this made you feel in the past and release any negative thoughts about yourself you associated with this experience you will continue to live in the cycle of what has been familiar and normal for you to experience. Often we spend time repeating the same patterns because at least these patterns fill up our time. They say that those who forget the past are doomed to repeat it. Rather, those who do not understand their past motivations will repeat it until they do. Take credit card debt, it's easier to just continue to fill a void you are experiencing in your life with shopping and racking up money on a credit card than to really look at your life. It's easier to tell yourself you just enjoy shopping instead of admitting there is something going on in your life that you're not dealing with effectively that is causing you to over consume material items that don't bring lasting joy. The cycle of overspending in this example can bring a temporary comfort to our lives to fill the void instead of doing the real work it would take to make significant changes in our lives to find out what the void is really all about.

To experience change we typically must give something else up in our lives. We are not always willing to give things up, sometimes out of habit and others out of not knowing what to replace the void with. This is a cycle that keeps people stuck for years or even decades. The important thing here is to start with looking at our thoughts about change. Before we can truly experience the change we want to make in our physical reality we must first begin with the thoughts in our head. Our mind likes to play tricks on us and tell us nothing can or will change. When we give into thinking this is true there will be no change in our realities. The only change that truly needs to be made is in what we believe is possible in our lives. If we think we can't stop shopping and racking up credit card debt then we probably won't reach our goal of having no credit card debt. When we can see the possibility of what it would look and feel like to be credit card debt free we may begin to take small steps towards reaching our goal. We live in circumstances of our own creating. Just as we created the debt we can also eliminate the debt if that becomes our primary focus. There is nothing too big for us to accomplish.

It comes down to the effort we are willing to exert in making those goals a reality. To do this we must engage in a different way of being, which we are not used to. For this to take place you must allow yourself to create a new mental image of who you are. To emerge as someone new and different you must first put away the image of who you think you are to make room for who you really are. If you're waking up every morning saying to yourself I'm bad with money then that is going to show up to support your conclusion about yourself. You will continue to make choices that support your idea that you're bad with money.

Credit card debt is only an example that I'm using. We could replace this example with anything and it would be the same concept. We should each take a moment to examine our own patterns and come up with ways in which we sabotage ourselves with our thinking patterns. The more you think positive thoughts about yourself and your situation the better life will be for you and those around you. We are wired to easily think negative thoughts about ourselves. It is important to evaluate the words we use with ourselves. Take one hour out of your day and pay attention to the thoughts that run through your mind. Are most of your thoughts positive and uplifting towards yourself or are they based in negativity and doubt?

Be honest with yourself here. Once the hour is up write down what you observed on a sheet of paper. What did you notice? Are there areas you could improve in? Do this for a few days without any judgment. Once you observe where your thoughts live you are able to shift from any negative thought patterns to more positive ones. Start taking back control of your thoughts and implement new healthy ones.

Using mantras and positive affirmations are great tools for turning your thoughts around. Set a goal for yourself in the direction you would like your thoughts to go and be gentle with yourself when negative thoughts creep in. Our brains need to be trained just like any muscle in our bodies. We wouldn't expect to have strong calf muscles if we never exercised them. The same thing goes with the brain. The more we practice positive thinking the easier positive thoughts will come to us. This is the biggest way to change how we experience the world around us. If you wake up and the first thought we think each morning is, "today will be a fantastic day", then chances are you will find evidence throughout your day that make it fantastic. Two people can experience the same thing and yet have two completely different ideas of what the experience was like all because of positive thought. When you are positive it makes life so much more enjoyable.

Deep within each of us we want the best experiences in life that we can have. People have completely changed their life circumstances by the power of positivity. It's a life force all its own and it's not just available to a lucky few. This type of life changing experience is available to each one of us. Once we begin to realize that we have more control it opens up a new way of living in the world. If this concept is too overwhelming for you and you don't know where to start then the best thing you can do for yourself is to start small. I look at this like running my marathon. I didn't start out running 26.2 miles. I started running one mile and then eventually two miles and so on. For some reason, we can understand this in terms of running, but we don't always understand it in terms of our overall lives.

So why don't we start? Most often because it takes effort. Living differently than we are now simply takes work. Sometimes it takes a lot of work and we tend to want to shy away from working hard, but if that is the attitude we take then we will get less than optimal results. The truth is we get one beautiful life and we don't know how long we will get to be here and experience it so you have two options. You can either show up halfway and get half the results and experiences or you can show up fully in your life and get a full life. It's up to you. What full looks like will be different for everyone, but what I have realized is when you commit to living an overflowing life you will never again be satisfied with living half full in whatever you decide to do. Whether it be in relationships, work, or hobbies. The interesting dynamic is if you find yourself going back to living half full you will be uncomfortable because you know you are capable of more. When you find yourself in this situation, after having lived a full life, you'll find yourself figuring out a way to live fully again. It's always there at your fingertips. It may feel like you must start all over again and chances are you might, but you'll find a way to get back to overflowing once again.

Part of letting go is coming to a place where you remember the reality of what was and stop romanticizing what you wanted it to be. Trust is at the root of healing. Trusting that things happen for a reason brings me great comfort.

We should be the gentlest and kindest to ourselves during times in our lives when we need healing the most. At least that's how I've felt during those times when my life has been rearranged leaving me searching for the light. A great healing thought is in knowing we always resurface as ourselves once again. That's the greatest part of having hope in our hearts. Hope cuts through the deadness of depression and shines light on the truth that we will exist once again in all our glory.

A few words of advice if you're going through a valley in your own life, get out in nature. Sitting inside ruminating about a loss, difficult experience, overwhelming feelings of anxiety or depression will only keep you locked in it. Getting out and about around the living is the key to processing the events that occur in our lives. We are one with nature. It is in our nature to return to our healthiest being when we are in Mother Nature. She sustains us, heals us, and enlivens our soul. If you are in a funk the first thing I would do is check in and ask yourself if you're getting enough movement through exercise, enough sun and enough of the calming embrace that nature provides freely and willingly to our souls. It helps to remember that life is best when we are able to be in balance and engaging with the world around us. Nature helps reset our focus along with quiet time with our Creator. I've never come across anyone who didn't benefit from going outside and playing. We need to allow ourselves to play more frequently like when we were kids. Even kids these days are losing their connection with the necessary tools in life that help instill peace into our sometimes chaotic lives. Television and video games, although entertaining, can often lead to isolation and comparing our lives to those on TV or in games, causing more harm than good. After my divorce, I had a lot of alone time on my hands and decided to shut off the TV and other unnecessary distractions. One very precious life-giving thing I found was when we go back to the basics of our lives and engage in activities that we loved growing up it makes our life simpler and more enjoyable. I took up riding my bike again and felt the old familiar tinge of happiness only the small things in life can bring.

I encourage anyone who is going through a painful situation to do something productive with your pain. This is the single biggest thing that will heal you. Using our own painful experiences to lift another during their pain is what ultimately comes back to us as healing. There isn't peace in wallowing. There is only more of the same. But be gentle with yourself until you are able to get to the place of giving back to others. You need your own amount of time and space to feel your own feelings. Then when you're ready, you may be open to giving back to others. Only after you've taken care of yourself first. In the beginning of grief there is typically large amounts of pain, sorrow, confusion, and dissolution to sift through before we start to feel like ourselves again. Seek out those who make you feel understood, comforted, and loved.

At the end of the day remember that you are also very powerful and have the ability to heal yourself. Sit with yourself, listen to the answers within your own heart about what may comfort you and talk with God as your best friend who knows you better than anyone. God knows how we will react to our triumphs and our tragedies as He made us and gave us our disposition, demeanor, and personality traits. When you're confused or feeling down share your load with Him, better yet just give it all to Him. He loves when you let Him help you.

You're not reduced by your experiences, you're enriched by them. There's no way our experiences reduce us. Even the ones we deem as negative show us something about ourselves. Perhaps it's our resiliency or our strength that wants to get our attention. Our ability to always choose ourselves in the end that enriches our lives. But to think we are somehow "less than" after having gone through an experience that helped shape us and show us more of who we are doesn't make sense. Experience teaches you more about your boundaries and enforcing them in the future, it's a win-win situation. When we are going through a dark time we are growing. Spiritual growth doesn't happen when everything stays the same. Being gentle with ourselves during these times of transition is the biggest gift we can give ourselves. I'm often reminded of the various seasons of our lives. We are given seasons of prosperity and seasons of wither, seasons of joy and seasons of deep sorrow, seasons of hope and seasons of despair. They are all there to teach us something.

On the topic of regret, my advice is not to have any. What's the point of regretting? We love to beat ourselves up. I am not a believer in mistakes. I believe that everything happens for a reason and that all decisions made led to our benefit, whether we recognize it at the time or not. Most things are fixable in life. Even the worst of circumstances may be turned around. Sometimes the only choice we have might be to move forward, but just because we can't go back and redo something doesn't make it a mistake. We are too hard on ourselves in this area and I believe God wants us to learn to be easier on ourselves and know that He will always be there to help us correct our path. When we think in terms of mistakes, we think that somehow we will never get out of the circumstance we are in. That's the wrong way to think, because once we get in this mindset it will be very difficult to get out of it and you will continue to perpetuate the same patterns.

True regret occurs when we want to do something we knew in our heart we could, but we still didn't do it. We all have probably heard that we regret the chances we didn't take the most not the things we did do. When we really look at it do we ever really regret trying? Even the things we tried that hurt or seem like a "failure" really aren't. We are all chasing the experience of being alive and when we stay still and stagnant we aren't really experiencing different ways of being. For some, it gets to a point where all we are doing is watching other people have the experiences we wish we were having. Then we wonder why we live our lives unfulfilled. It's because we are looking at others doing things we ourselves were put here on Earth to do. God created our interests to be unique to each one of us. Some were born with a desire to play an instrument while others were born with a desire to paint or connect with people; so when we see other people doing what we ourselves want to be doing it creates a longing in our own souls, which then creates discontentment. Instead of going out and doing the things we want to be doing we sit back and let time pass listening to all the reasons it won't work out for us. We see those who are out doing what we want to be doing as somehow more gifted, talented, or special than we are when in truth they aren't. They are just out there taking action and doing it.

What we are doing in these situations is comparing ourselves to others and this is never a healthy path to go down. Comparison thinking only hurts our potential. We can get so caught up in our negative self-talk and comparison thinking that we don't give ourselves enough leeway to go and be the best we can be. If you really want something bad enough, and it is meaningful enough for you to take the first step, then by sticking with it you will have given yourself the most beautiful experience in the world by giving yourself the experience of being who you were meant to be. This takes effort and a choice on your part to really challenge yourself to become a higher version of yourself. Real, true, deep change can be a hard thing for anyone to go through, but transformation will never occur if you don't at least try to become the person you know deep down you were meant to evolve into.

Regret compounds on itself the longer you don't try doing what you really knew in your heart you wanted to do. Years of regret can add up later in life to the point where you grow sick and tired from never really trying. We must release the regret we have for our past to wash the slate clean and move forward. If we continue to carry regret in our lives we will never take that first step. We will always be stuck in the belief that since we haven't started yet we will never be able to begin. Instead if we can shift our thinking to a more forgiving state of mind we can see that we weren't ready to take the first step until now.

This frees up our energy to live in the moment. One of life's greatest gifts is the gift of being able to begin at any point we choose. You don't have to even question why things turned out the way they did in the past or why you didn't try something you wanted to try. If we can truly accept our past for what it was, with compassion for ourselves, we are able to see that everything that occurred was for a reason. If you hadn't made the choices you made in the past you wouldn't have learned the beautiful lessons life was trying to teach you at that time.

As you move beyond where you've been you start to experience different aspects of your true nature and will begin to realize all that you are capable of. This is what makes life fun and interesting to live. We confuse our past with our present too often and that doesn't allow us the space to be who we are today without the confines and shackles of yesterday or the anxiousness of tomorrow. What if I told you, you are completely whole and complete within your flaws and imperfections, that in fact those flaws and imperfections you see are what makes you completely perfect in the eyes of God? God wants to experience life through you and gets so much joy out of you being exactly who you are. We put so much pressure on ourselves to be perfect when in reality that is not the point of living. The point of life is to be flawed, but still being able to decide to wake up each day and try your hardest to be the best version of ourselves. There is nothing wrong with our imperfections except for our mindset around them. If we were each able to get to a place where we listened to our doubts about who we think we are less and the truth about who we really are, our lives would be a much more pleasurable experience for each of us as well as the collective.

When you decide to wake up and be loved then you inevitably are going to bring love to each interaction you make along your daily path. The energy you bring to life is emitted to all other living things you encounter so it becomes a choice. Sometimes it is a minute by minute, second by second choice about who you want to show up and be when you are around your family, co-workers, and everyone you encounter in-between. Have you ever noticed how quickly someone who walks into a room with negative energy can shift the vibe in the room? Now how about someone who walks in with an uplifting, positive energy? It makes all the difference in the world. When you encounter different energies that show up it will be your decision to either protect the energy surrounding you or pick up the energy of others. Realize that it is not your responsibility to carry the weight of others. When individuals are upset and unhappy in their lives you do not have to take the energy they are emanating as your own.

Often people get affected by the attitudes or opinions of others. This is such a shame because it has nothing to do with you. Their attitude is about them and when we mistakenly think it's a reflection of us we begin to let others shape who we are instead of separating ourselves from their negative thinking. Don't let someone make you feel bad about yourself, instead it is important to separate that person's inability to be positive from your own self-worth. It is very dangerous territory when we allow someone to inhibit our self-confidence. We are all here with the ability to accomplish great things. When we surround ourselves with negative people it will diminish our ability to live in a world where all things are possible for ourselves.

It is extremely important to surround yourself with people who will uplift you. It is necessary if you are going to experience the life you want to experience. Eventually you will become keenly aware of how other people's energy may affect your own. To reach your highest self it will become important for you to be protective about the people you allow into your life. This may feel selfish at first, but as you grow on the path towards enlightenment you will come to understand and accept that you are here to take care of yourself first and foremost. Part of taking care of yourself becomes about who you keep close to you. Your own beautiful soul is the only one you are responsible for throughout your journey. Whatever you need to do to ensure its safety, health, and wellbeing will become of utmost importance. We are taught to believe we should put everyone else's needs above our own no matter the price. No wonder so many people end up being depressed when we constantly put our own desires, wants, and needs at the bottom of the list. The focus should then become about empowering others to reach their own levels of happiness versus taking their happiness on for them.

Making peace with our past is the greatest gift towards healing we can give ourselves and those around us. Sometimes we stuff so many experiences in our pocket along our journey that we get weighed down by all that's happened in our lives. We forget that all we need to do in any moment is to simply pause to set all the past pain and hurt down. We get so caught up in feeling like there was another path we should have taken or that things in our life didn't turn out the way they should have. But what is "should have" anyways?

You are always right where you are supposed to be. The Universe is always giving you exactly what you need when you need it for your learning. During my single days, I knew there were people who were meant to cross my path, meant to be a part of my journey and I theirs. Crossings that wouldn't have happened if I would have chosen any other path. The breaking points of our lives are the points at which we can no longer continue down the path we are on. This is a very spiritual decision even if we don't recognize it as such at the time. It's similar to a butterfly. The butterfly stays in its cocoon for the length of time it's meant to while it needs the comforts of safety. What would happen to the butterfly if it never left its cocoon? It would never feel the liberation of flight. We are much like the butterfly. We build up to the point where we can take flight and chart our own course. When you get to the point where you no longer desire to feel the pressures of living in your own confinement you too will break free just like the butterfly. But first the cocoon must make sure it has given the butterfly sufficient time to heal all its butterfly parts because it knows this is the only way the butterfly will spread its wings to take flight. Like the caterpillar in the cocoon, you will take flight in a beauty all your own.

Chapter Eleven

Who Am I?

Phenomenal Woman
By Maya Angelou

It's the fire in my eyes,
And the flash of my teeth,
The swing in my waist,
And the joy in my feet.
I'm a woman.
Phenomenally.
Phenomenal woman,
That's me.

I've thought long and hard about how I wanted to end my book and what keeps coming back to me is that I want to speak directly to your heart. I want to tell you everything I've learned, I want to breathe all my life into yours, to give you the knowing that you can do anything you want with your life whether you've ever been told so or not. I want you to be at peace with your own story, and know that you have the power to recreate all the parts and pieces that still feel rough around the edges. Most importantly, I want to tell you to live, to never give up on yourself, and to keep the sparkle alive within your own soul. To walk in faith is to believe that everything you are faced with is for your good, leading you towards something beautiful if only up on the horizon. The dark days are there as your greatest and most sacred teacher. They show you your strength, your resilience, your determination and give you a big capacity to love and be loved. You are not fragile, if you were, you wouldn't have signed up to come here. Earth is a far denser energy and place to inhabit.

One of my all-time favorite quotes is by Pierre Teilhard de Chardin where he says, "We are not human beings having a spiritual experience. We are spiritual beings having a human experience." I'll never forget the first time I read this quote, it resonated so deeply within me that I longed to remember who I was before I came here. If you believe in past lives and the progression of each life enhancing our souls I hope you will also resonate with this quote. In this day and age, we are having such difficulty mixing the soul self with the worldly self that it becomes the human aspect of who we are right now. The human self presents many more challenges than the soul self. The soul knows who it is, the human self is always searching to find its way. The soul is limitless. The human condition is full of limitations.

I remember being at the beginning of my spiritual awakening, again in gratitude to my dad for giving me something very real and significant to search for, in essence I craved to know where he went after he left his earthly body. In the searching I found more than I bargained for, I found my truth, that he was still with me and always would be. The only thing that separates us is the physical and nonphysical world. It's often referred to as the veil. And that's just it, a very thin veil is all that separates us. It breaks my heart when I hear people question where their loved ones go. Most likely because I felt that yearning, that feeling of nothingness, after he was gone. But as I've walked my path I learned for myself my dad is all around, I've been given more signs than one deserves and I'm grateful for each one. It's been years since I've questioned where loved ones go. The biggest comfort is in knowing the body dies, but love endures forever. There is no ending to the love. Love is what always was and what will always remain.

Don't be afraid of dying, be afraid of not living while you're here.

I often look at death as an elevation of our spirit to a higher realm, one we cannot fully fathom with our human brain. If you've ever wondered if your loved one is near ask them for a sign and you will surely receive it. Part of the receiving is being open to the message. Don't shut yourself off to believing. I've heard some say they don't believe because what if they're wrong or what if it sounds crazy. I went through this same struggle for quite some time before I realized that a life worth living is one where I believe in miracles. We don't just go into nothingness, but that we are transformed in to spirit once again where we are weightless, limitless, and free. There are times I crave the spiritual experiences because they show me glimpses of Heaven on Earth. They are around us all the time if we are open enough to allow them. Notice how something makes you feel. The thought of there being nothing after here probably makes you feel heavy, fearful, and depressed. When you take the opposite, and think about being reunited with your greatest love, your Creator, and being reunited with all of your loved ones you probably feel a deep sense of joy. Our emotions are guided by our beliefs.

I want you to know that you have it all within you. You never need to look to anyone else for your own answers. It's all within you. Make your life your own. Shape it and color it with all your favorite things. Don't take no for an answer. Keep going, never lose sight of who you are. When things enter your life that don't jive with your energy and what you want for yourself let them go as fast as they came into your life. Your life is up to you. Do you want a small life or a big life? Do you want to have faith and seek the light? These are all choices you have within your control. The realization that we are much more in control of our existence than we let on is both empowering and overwhelming, beautiful and scary. It suggests that there really isn't a dream that's off the table. If there is something you long to do there is a way to do it. You may have obstacles along the way and it will require patience and hard work, but it's possible. It's better to live with a heart wide open than one that's closed off to possibility. Life is meant to be savored and lived like a love story between you and yourself.

Have you ever given up on a dream you once cherished? Did you take time off because of life's inevitable distractions? Were you caught up in fear? Well, it's time to get back in the game, darling. Don't let defeat win. Rise and claim your victory over life's roadblocks. You're not the first one who's suffered trials along the way to success and you won't be the last. Your story is still unfolding, don't let it unfold in the direction of someone else's longing. Let it sprout wings and fly in the direction of your truest destiny. Your life was written in the stars long ago and there is nothing you can do to make it not so.

Facing my dad's death has been the biggest challenge of my life. It opened up a whisper so deep inside of me I couldn't put it at bay. I had to look for the silver lining or I wouldn't be able to overcome what felt so tragic. If we are each fortunate enough there will come a time in our lives where we have no other choice but to dig deep within and ask the questions that make life meaningful. Who am I? Why am I here? What is my purpose? How do I live my most fulfilling life? How do I grow closer to God? These are all questions that my dad's passing led me to ask. Questions that I never would have stumbled upon if my entire world hadn't been uprooted. Or at least I wouldn't have stumbled upon them so soon. The thing about God is He enjoys watching us search, in many ways, for Him knowing our search is always in an effort to find Him at the end of every road we've taken.

I've found God in all sorts of ways, by running on the trail trying to run out my demons, sitting in the middle of a forest on top of a mountain in Colorado at an Ashram, having Sunday morning coffee and a chat at my dad's grave, crossing the finish line of a marathon, looking out over Big Sur on one of my solo soul trips. But most importantly I've found Him in the good deeds I do for others, in the relentless prayers I prayed over and over each time my life went through a major shift and in the nights that were so lonely they left me feeling desperate for connection. I've found Him in the beaming sun on a seemingly perfect day and in the dark shallows of my own wailing cries of despair when it seemed depression was going to cast its net on me for good. I've found Him in the laughter of my nephews and nieces and in the love from my family. I've found Him in the glimmering hope of knowing that the dawn always comes again. There is a new day awaiting right around the corner, and if we choose to do our work and feel the pain of loss and misunderstandings of what life is and is not, we will find our way back to the place of rest that is promised.

We will go through hardships. For some it might be the loss of a loved one, a relationship that ended before we wanted it to, or a job that didn't work out. When we take our hard-won life lessons and begin to integrate them into our lives allowing them to have an impact on our choices and the way we choose to live our lives, we show the Universe we've got the lesson. In this "showing" or display of lessons learned, we no longer attract in our lives that which needed to be learned. We in turn become free of the lesson and ready to move on to the next level with a deeper understanding and more thoughtful approach to how we conduct our lives.

It's in our hands how long we want to live in the same old patterns. We will ascend to a higher level of consciousness by allowing our lessons to refine us, to attract what we truly desire in to our lives. Keep at it, and you'll surely get where you're meant to go. We never know what a loss will end up creating in our lives. We tend to look at a loss as if something won't come along to replace that which we no longer have. There's always something that fills in the gap. When I look back on my marriage and everything I experienced after, I can clearly see the Universe stepped in and helped me fill the gap with so many things that felt like me. I was a willing participant in creating a beautiful life for myself full of the things I love the most. Finding the great joys of being an auntie and spending time with family has always been a high priority in my life. In the gap is where I found myself through running, yoga and taking long bike rides with God. Talking to Him about all my hopes and dreams and working through the hurt and pain of losing my dad, wanting to live a life I could look back on and feel proud of. I needed solace and peace in my life to heal from the pain of so much loss in a short period of time. The gap helped me do that.

On an intuitive level, we know what we need. There are times where we get caught up in destructive patterns pulling ourselves away from what will help us heal. Sometimes we just don't have the energy or the capacity to keep up the pace at which most of us are comfortable living. We are more comfortable with running around "doing" instead of sitting in quiet contemplation. The quiet is deafening and reveals to us what we get away with not hearing throughout the day. Things that would cause us to change the way we are living. As I've aged my dreams have become even more fragile like watching time slip through an hourglass, knowing I won't be here forever. The reality we live in on this Earth is that the more we put the very things off that mean the most to us the deeper they get buried in our souls and the less likely they are to surface. If you have let your dreams die it's time to bring them back to life. Don't let your dreams die with you, let them be lived out loud while you're here.

One of my favorite places to go is the cemetery where my dad, grandmas and grandpas are laid to rest. I'm drawn there on happy occasions just as much as I am on sad ones. I love sitting next to my loved ones' graves to catch up and spend time with each of them. I feel a sense of peace there. As if all the spirits that have gone before me are cheering me on, perhaps pushing me to live life differently than they did. This last winter I was out at the cemetery visiting my dad and I looked around at all the gravestones and thought about the lives they lived before leading them to their graves. I wondered if they lived the life they dreamed of or if they settled for the one they were given. I wondered if any of them had a spirit like mine where they longed so fervently to touch other people's lives in an effort to make their own more meaningful. But more than anything I feel a sense of support at the cemetery, that the ones who surround us in spirit are cheering us on, my loved ones on the other side are there to support me and that's a wonderful feeling.

During the times in my life where I've really had to dig deep inside of myself to keep going down the road less traveled, when I couldn't muster the strength for myself, I think about my dad, and my grandmas and grandpas, and I do it for them. It's important to remember why we do what we do, what's your reason behind what it is you want to do with your life? We can get distracted by all the noise in our heads as we tend to the business of our lives. It's important to have your "why" to come back to. Without your "why" there would be no point in moving forward along the path.

It's taken me years to write this book. In the process I would get distracted, I would get caught up in fear of putting myself out there. When I would get distracted I would come back to "why" I was writing this book. It took the energy of fear away and replaced it with the energy of love. I've had to remind myself over and over again that I'm sharing my story for my dad and to help others through their own painful journey of loss. This is what our "why" should do. It's all about falling more in love with our dreams than our fears. I want to live purposefully in an effort to use all the time I have left to experience things my crossed over loved ones never got to. In doing so they get to experience it with me and I allow their death to be the very thing that propels me forward and encourages me to not be afraid.

We are all here for a short time, whether we were afraid or had anxiety while we did the things that were most important to us will matter very little. What will matter the most is that we did it. I am reminded of an article I read a few years ago that was about talking to the dying about their biggest regrets in life. Their regrets included things like not really going for it, or working too much, or being afraid of their dreams. Instead of allowing that to haunt me I use it as motivation to recognize when I'm falling into those traps that are easy to find ourselves in. One way in which we feel like we have lived is by stopping to show gratitude for our journey. The small things in life add up to be the big things. Walking outside in the evening to watch the sunset, listening to the sound of crickets, or watching fireflies are among the sweetest memories to cherish. Intentions are great, but if the follow through is not there it remains unlived. It's in the setting of intention and the follow through that brings peace to our souls.

I suddenly realized my quest and search had one underlying question that encompassed it all, Who Am I? This is a question I have asked myself often over the years, at various points in my life. Who Am I? And I suppose the answer has changed some along the way. It seems I've collected different phrases at various points in my life as many of us have. At one point I was a child, I've always been a daughter, then a wife, eventually a divorced woman making it on her own and somewhere along the way I was a student and a teacher of others. A woman, yet still a girl in some ways. What do all those words even say about me? In my opinion, they say very little about who I really am. They are simple terms we use to identify ourselves. I was once again left with WHO AM I? Outside of all the labels society wants to put on us, or at times we want to put on ourselves to feel more comfortable in our own skin, I wanted to look deeper to find my answer. Living in a world that can be hard to understand didn't provide me with any clearer answers, which led me to the same question again, really Who Am I? Well I took that leap of faith. I stepped outside of my comfort zone to try to find the real me. And surprisingly enough I loved finding who I really am. I left everything behind. A good job, a stable life with friends and family surrounding me. The picture perfect American Dream. I left it ALL. And what I found surprised me. My ultimate truth is: I'm a child of God.

As I sit in meditation I find the real me. When I sit alone on a mountaintop with nothing around me except God and a steady breeze is where I find myself. As I run mile after mile I find who I am. They are all me. Every last one of them is me. And they are all beautiful. I'm dedication, I'm commitment, and more than anything, I am love. Don't you dare hide your greatness underneath false clothing. Be big. Be bold. Own it. Be who you were created to be. You. We should all ask ourselves who we are. We get so preoccupied and wrapped up in what everyone else thinks of us that we seldom sit back and ask ourselves what we think. How many times have you listened to someone else's perspective of who you are and what you are made of or what you are meant to be doing here instead of just listening to yourself? Life's too short to give more credence to what the co-worker in the cube over thinks of you. Believe in yourself first and you will be amazed at how your life changes right before your very eyes. We've all seen it. People who take chances and go off on their own journey leaving everything behind in the quest to find themselves. What they share after their quest is amazing. I hope this book has encouraged you to find out who you are and to take the challenges in life as the sweetest invitation you will ever receive to look deeper at who you are and then have the courage to go find the answer.

And now these three remain: faith, hope and love.
But the greatest of these is love.
1 Corinthians 13:13

The biggest piece of my longing to write this book was as a gift to my dad. If I could write anything about my dad it would be how lucky I felt that he was mine. I am one lucky girl that God chose him to be my daddy. I'll never forget the time when I was about ten years old and I stubbed my toe in the middle of the night and there was my dad coming to the rescue, to bring his crying little girl back to bed. You see my dad had a sweet, sentimental side, but boy was my dad funny. His silly side never went away no matter how old he got, which was one of the things I loved about him most.

My dad taught me so many lessons about life, some of which I learned once he was no longer here. The thing I remember most is how much he loved me. I'll never forget the simple ways he showed it and how much each one meant to me. The simple things in life always mean the most. Like the time I got into a minor car accident on the way to school during my junior year of high school. I hadn't been driving all that long. As I was turning to make my way up a hill, I wasn't paying attention as well as I should have been and accidentally ran the front right tire into the gutter, spinning the car around, smashing the rim and flattening the tire. I couldn't believe what I had just done and all I could do was start bawling. Luckily, a nice gentleman who worked for the power company offered to drive me home to tell my dad what had happened. As I climbed in the passenger seat I told the man I was so worried that my dad would be angry with me and I'd get in big trouble. I was anxious as I ran up the stairs outside of our house and flung open the door to tell my dad what had happened.

A sigh of relief came over me after the first words out of his mouth were, "are you okay?" As I said "yes" his next question was, "did you hurt anyone else?" After I said "no" his response still makes me feel loved today. He said, "then it's no big deal, Angie, accidents happen, it's just a car. A car can be replaced but you can't." I don't know why I expected him to be so upset with me, but when he wasn't I realized this is how I wanted to be when accidents happened in life. I wanted to be forgiving and kind. I still laugh at how big of an accident I made it in my head and how little it all was to my dad. When we got to the car I remember him laughing at my exaggerated reaction saying, "this is no big deal, all I have to do is change the tire." That small incident was much bigger to me than my dad even knew. His response made me feel loved and safe. The car didn't matter to my dad, I did. I remember feeling surprised about how my dad reacted, but most importantly I remember feeling lucky he was my dad. We laughed about this memory for years to come.

A loved one with a life well lived will continue to teach you even after their gone. I appreciated all my dad taught me as much as I could while he was here, but far more when he wasn't around in physical form any longer. A lot of people have asked me what propelled me to deal with losing my dad the way I have, to use it as a catalyst for a better life. To be honest, I can't answer exactly why some people take loss and let it break them, never returning to the wholeness of who they once were, and why others turn the loss into their greatest motivator to live a more meaningful life. I do know that I always wanted to do something great with my life and until losing my dad I didn't know exactly what that "something" was. I've always helped people, gotten behind a good cause, and felt a sense of purpose by giving a helping hand to someone who could use it. But that still doesn't get at the hidden truth within the question. For me, if I can help others with grief it feels like my life has more meaning and losing my dad didn't happen for no reason at all. I can somehow keep him alive longer and somewhere inside of me. I need to do that for myself to make sense out of it. If I can be better in some way, help even one person believe in themselves, heal something that feels really broken, or just have a small iota of faith again that things do happen for a reason and that they'll be okay, that they'll live again, and be happy again, then it feels like the pain of losing my dad was for something. When I keep my dad alive in myself and in helping others with what his death has taught me there's meaning. When I share my pain, I share him. I share our love.

That's the biggest gift we each have on this Earth. To give love and to receive love. Love is not even, it is not this for that, it's unconditional love that's the greatest gift of all. It's loving someone for all their beautiful parts that are effortless to love and for all their ugly parts that are painful to accept, because they somehow say something about ourselves. My dad was one of those people who was just plain easy to love. He was endearing in so many ways. Our love for one another remains. I can still feel his love surround me. I have no doubt that in Heaven people know how much he's loved back here on Earth. There's a bond between Heaven and Earth that is never severed, it's here, all around us. The older I get the closer I get to seeing him again and that gives me great peace about aging myself, knowing I will go where he is and he'll be there welcoming me home.

I'll never forget the last moment I had with my dad alone. It was a very sweet, tender moment, filled with love. I've wondered if he somehow knew his time was coming, that God was going to part the skies and call him home. I think he did know on some level and I think he was okay with it. Because at the end of the day my dad knew who he was, he was a good man. He knew who God was. And in his own words, one of the most beautiful things I've ever heard in my life came out of my dad's understanding of life during a time when I was very lost. During another great loss of my life, after losing my dear Grandma Alice, my dad held me in his arms, wiped away tears from my eyes and said wisely, "Don't be upset baby, the most beautiful part of living is dying. We all must live and we all must die. It's the circle of life." My dad knew without a doubt that our best day on this Earth is our last. It brings us home to our reunion on the other side to be with God again. Remembering this reminds me of how special my dad truly was. He didn't fret or worry about much. He was laid back and trusting. Maybe he'd come to terms with what life was and wasn't long before he comforted me that day, but that moment changed my life forever with his view of death. This was one of the greatest gifts a father could give a daughter. To know even after they're gone they're at home with their Maker once again.

The Road that Led Me Home to Myself

The relief that surrounded me when I made the final decision to move back home to Nebraska is something I will never forget. I was done in Colorado. All I wanted was to go back where I belonged, to those who loved me and those I loved the most. I prayed to God the day before moving back home, in that close to desperate way we can find ourselves in, that this dark time had to have been for something. That I didn't just give up my life in Nebraska for nothing, but that something good would ultimately come out of the deep grief I had been in for the past six months. My biggest prayer that day was that I would meet the love of my life on the other side of this move back home. I asked God to help me meet my twin flame. I had learned about this concept while in Colorado and longed to meet mine. This little talk I had with God unfolded a few weeks later in a way that I never would have imagined.

I've learned God delights in surprising us. Several weeks after returning home I walked into a little grocery store in the small town I grew up in only to find the love of my life standing at a magazine rack with his back towards me. A feeling from the pit of my stomach bubbled up inside of me, telling me that I knew him from many lives before. I had only met him a few months earlier during a chance encounter and had exchanged several work-related emails back and forth over the course of the past few months, but nothing personal was discussed. I sure didn't expect to find him standing a few feet in front of me sifting through magazines on Easter Sunday. I was briefly stopping in to say "hello" to my mother at a store I hadn't stepped foot into in over five years in a town I moved from years ago only to find God had a much bigger plan in mind for my quick visit.

In my most excited voice I approached him and said, "Hi there." He turned around slowly to greet me with a smile as if acknowledging that both of us had been searching for something more than a magazine that day. We just happened to find it on Easter Sunday, of all days. I excitedly rushed over to have a chat with the biggest surprise of my day, asking him what he was doing here, him answering me, that he lives two blocks down the road and then him switching the conversation to asking me what I was doing here since I live in Denver. My response back was that I had just moved back a few weeks earlier and that I grew up in this town and then introduced him to my mom. As he gave me his number and walked out the door I couldn't help but smile knowing this was planned by God with our own soul agreement many moons ago. Every time I look back on that day I am reminded of how intricate our lives are and that there's always a plan even when we don't see it. Sometimes God gives us the biggest gift of our lives in the aisle of a grocery store. I knew God had work for us to do together. Only time would tell where that day would lead us, but one thing was certain I was ready to find out.

A few months after returning home I began to realize that my journey to Colorado was more about self-acceptance than anything else. I needed to leave to be able to return with a new appreciation for what I already had. There was no longer this whisper in my ear that there was somewhere better or more "me" waiting to be discovered. After returning home I fully realized the true value of growing up in that small town being surrounded by family and friends who I adored. And that God had a plan the entire time by putting a Mississippi man in that small Nebraska town. We were meant to meet it was only a matter of time.

God kept showing me little by little that I already had a home and I could come back to it any time I wanted, but that my real home was with Him. He also showed me I may wander, but I'm never lost. I no longer wanted to change my surroundings once I accepted who I was on the inside. I love her and now she knows it.

Prayers of Hope

A prayer for strength & guidance

Father God,

You are my strength, my fortress, my love, my blessings and my best friend. Thank You for the blessings You have bestowed upon my life. Shower Your infinite strength upon my life allowing me to know that what I'm going through will make me stronger, wiser and more able to move forward in the direction You are calling me to go. When I get discouraged remind me that in You all things are possible.

In Your name I pray,

Amen

A prayer for purpose

Lord Jesus,

You know my heart, You know me better than anyone else ever could. You know my desires to live my life on purpose, to use the gifts You have generously given me to make this world a better place. I pray for You to reveal my purpose to me now so that I may walk in Your love and light to uplift the planet and those around me. I am now open to the gifts You have given me and willing to listen as You speak Your truth to me.

Thank you, Father, for loving and guiding me.

Amen

A prayer for the broken hearted

God,

Show me the way, show me my path, allow me to forgive those who I feel have wronged me and hurt my heart. Give me Your peace where I have none and allow me to prosper despite the situation I'm in. Give me Your perspective so that I may be freed of my human way of looking at this situation. Through You I am free and all things are possible. Allow my heart to be open to wanting the best for all others. Give me Your solace, refuge and understanding during this season of my life and forevermore.

In Your loving embrace I am free.

Amen

A prayer to remove obstacles

O Lord Jesus,

I am feeling stuck, immobile and as if I've lost my way. I know You are the way maker, the barrier remover and the soul booster. I come to You today with my heart emptied and my spirit humbled to ask You to release any blocks that stand in my way of finding my true self, my most authentic path to finding the place on Earth where Heaven meets me where I am. I long to live a life of fulfillment, joy and peace. Please, Father, help me to find my way. If I have gotten off the path gently put me back on the path You have chosen for my life. Remove situations and circumstances that are not of my highest good. And replace it with Your will for my life.

In Jesus' name,

Amen

A prayer for self-love and acceptance

God,

Allow my heart to stay intact, my soul to know the truth, and my spirit to keep on shining.
Allow me to be strong in who I am while living in a world that seeks to change me.
Allow me to be steadfast and heart-strong to the real reason I'm here for love, compassion and a spirit of generosity.
Allow me to reach for my dreams, live my purpose and love who I am.
Allow my challenges to be turned into triumphs, my wounds to be turned into forgiveness and my disappointments to be turned into wisdom.
Allow my soul to be still and my story to reflect who I really am.
Allow others to view me as a masterpiece of Your creation.
Allow my place in the world to be revealed.
Allow me to accept my brilliance and ward off any negativity that comes my direction.
Allow me to come home to You each and every night knowing I've found You and that's all that really matters.

You are my everything.

Amen

A prayer of thanks

Lord,

Thank You for my life, for my passions, for my family and my friends. Thank You for work that keeps me busy, love that keeps me warm and faith that keeps me going. You have blessed me beyond measure, I am eternally grateful for the breath I take, for the sights I see and for the laughter when it comes. You are my joy.

Thank you for making me, me.

Amen

A prayer for healing

Father God,

You know the tragedies of my life and the pain associated with them. (Take a moment to tell God the specific wounds you would like healed). Please, Lord Jesus, free me from the wreckage these wounds have caused. Make my spirit whole once again. Take these ashes and raise me to new and beautiful heights. Give me perseverance to overcome life's challenges and a fresh path to walk that will lead me ultimately home to You.

In Jesus' name,

Amen

Pretty Little Things From My Heart to Yours

The Night

When the night is settled and the day is done are you going to be able to say you won?

When the dark is upon you and there is no light in sight what are you going to cling to in the night?

When laughter is a distant memory, like an old friend, who are you going to reach your hand out to, to help you mend?

When you're all you have who are you going to become?

Look within, you were always there helping yourself until the very end.

Dear One,

You continue to believe, okay? Don't let this darkness overtake you forever. Feel free to have hope again. Hope is what will help you the most right now. Believe that better times are yet to come. You've got to believe, precious one. There's so much more around the corner. There always is.

God loves you. He always has and He always will. Nothing will change that. This is just a season and all seasons must come to an end. Start by loving yourself more and all else will fall into place. You're okay just as you are. Life is okay just as it is. You will make it. Don't you worry, you will make it. This is not the end of the story. It never is.

The reality is life goes on. Make sure you go with it. It doesn't wait for us to be ready. It will pass with or without you. Don't let it get you stuck for too long. You're meant to go with it where it wants to take you, it has things to show you. Get out in it, enjoy it, live it up!

When you have big dreams you can also have big disappointments. Don't let those disappointments define you. Learn from them. And then try again.

When times get tough you keep on going. Pick yourself up, dust yourself off and keep on trucking. Don't allow the sorrows of yesterday to determine your happiness today. Life is a beautiful, messy ride. Keep on striving for what it is you desire in life. Never give up. Giving up would only be giving up on yourself and you just can't do that. Go out and prove to yourself that you've got what it takes. Even when your fears want to take over, keep going.

Love

Love yourself to the very end.
Love yourself in your brokenness, in your sadness, in your frustration.
It's all you.
All of it was there to teach you something.
Take the lessons and forget the rest.

The Journey

There will be times you lose yourself, where you don't know who you are.

Keep looking, keep finding yourself. Don't lose yourself to the ways of this world.

Delight in the small things. Soak up the sun. Drown out the noise. Listen to your heart. Say a big hearty "yes" to your adventure. Let go of control. Take life slow. Right your wrongs. Go with the flow. Shine your light. Give compassion to your dark. Speak your truth. Know your worth. Claim your path. Chart your course. When you need to start over don't be discouraged. Believe in yourself. Keep your head held high. Use your voice. Let your eyes sparkle and your soul come alive. Keep the faith. Love yourself. Don't look outside of yourself for what you need. Believe in your story. Count your lucky stars. Accept your greatness. Live your dreams. Be you.

Wings

You are set free to fly
Fly high above the sky now
Never asking why
Your time has come to be weightless
Don't carry your burden for another day
Life was never supposed to be that way
Go on now, be free
Be free
Be free
Do you hear the whispering winds
They are calling you forth
The only thing they care to know is why you came here
Make sure you listen to your whispering winds
And fly free

Afterword from the Author

During the editing of my book another loss hit close to my heart. My Uncle Dan, my dad's twin, unexpectedly passed away a short three months before sending in the final version of my book to my publishing company. To say my Uncle Dan was a second dad to me is an understatement. I wouldn't have been able to get through the loss of my dad without him by my side.

What do you do when pain comes knocking on your door once again? You keep going. You keep going for the ones you've lost. You keep going for the love you shared with them. You keep going for God. My Uncle Dan was the closest person I had to my dad here on Earth. Knowing he's reunited with my dad once again gives me peace and joy yet it is so hard to say, "until we meet again." And the grief continues…

When you're struggling with one loss and another is thrown in within a short time it knocks the wind right out of your sails. Two months after my Uncle Dan went to be with God in Heaven, another close Uncle of mine passed away unexpectedly, my Uncle Steve. My Uncle Steve wasn't only family, he was good friends with my Uncle Dan and my dad, all graduating high school together. Now they are all flying high with the Angels. My Uncle Steve had a grin that would light up a room and a singing voice that would melt your heart.

I'll always love and remember them both for the important roles they played in my life after my dad passed away as each of my Uncles have. I'll keep them with me in my heart as I move forward on my journey to help others heal from loss.

Remember, I don't just speak these words, I live them. I, too, have loved and lost. My heart is with you, my dear reader, as we will never live in a world where people aren't taken away. What gets me through? My faith. My certainty that God's at the helm. My faith in Him allows me to rest in peace, between the sobbing and the crying out for my loved ones moving on from this life, into their eternal life with God. I know they're in a better place than we can even imagine and that I will be there with them one day myself. Until that day comes I will continue to honor God by helping others grieve. Never let anyone mess with your faith, it's the most precious gift we're given.

In the end if you remember only one thing, remember life is fragile, we never know when God will come calling for someone we love to come Home. God's timing isn't always our timing, but it doesn't mean it isn't perfect timing. Each day love as if it's the last time you'll see your loved ones, hug them as if it's your last gift to them. Life is short, love harder.

Forgive easily, love unconditionally. We all have something we're aching over. In the end, be gentle and kind. Life is an assortment of experiences with them all leading us to the same place. As Ram Dass said, "we're all just walking each other home."